Asante Twi Learner's Dictionary

Asante Twi Pronunciations in Akan-English &

English-Akan

kasahorow

Designed in Africa
Revised 2019-07-27

Efia N.

Dea ɛ wɔ mu

1

Preface

Hello! We created this learner's dictionary to help you read Modern Akan! Keep it by your side when reading English and Akan books.

If you are reading and you never have to use a dictionary, then it means you are ready to read more advanced texts! Well done!

Here are some words used in this dictionary to show you the function of the word in a sentence:

Word	Meaning
nom	A *noun* is a name
adj	An *adjective* shows the quality of a noun
pro	A *pronoun* points to a noun
act	A *verb* is an action
adv	An *adverb* shows the intensity of a verb
sci	A *scientific* term
math	A *mathematics* term

We wish you many happy reading adventures in English and Akan!

kasahorow Editors

Asante Twi - English

Entries in the Asante Twi - English section are arranged in this order:

a b d e ɛ f g h i j k l m n o ɔ p r s t u v w y z

Ø
a//

a
that/-a/

a
a/-a/

a-ɛ-da-mu-soronko
unique/-a-e-r-d-a-m-u-s-o-r-o-n-k-o/

a-ɛ-di-akyiri
last/-a-e-r-d-i-a-ch-i-r-i/

a-ɛ-di-kan
first/-a-er-d-i-k-a-n/

a-ɛ-wɔ-abotare
patient/-a-e-r-w-o-r-a-b-o-t-a-r-e/

a-kɔm-de-no
hungry/-a-k-or-m-d-e-n-o/

a-ɔ
that/-a-or/

a-ɔ-fɛre-ade
shy/-a-o-r-f-e-r-r-e-a-d-e/

a-ɔ-nnyi-awiei
eternal/-a-or-n-n-i-a-w-i-e-i/

a-ɔkyɛso
gracious/-a-or-ch-er-s-o/

aa
ah/-a-a/

aagɔn
argon/-a-a-g-or-n/

aaha
no/-a-a-h-a/

aane
yes/-a-a-n-e/

abaa
whip/-a-b-a-a/

abaawa
maid/-a-b-a-a-w-a/

abaayewa
maiden/-a-b-a-a-y-e-w-a/

abae
cane/-a-b-a-e/

abaeforo
novice/-a-b-a-e-f-o-r-o/

abaeforo
modern/-a-b-a-e-f-o-r-o/

abakan
firstborn/-a-b-a-s-a-n-t-e -t-w-i/

abakyiba
lastborn/-a-b-a-ch-i-b-a/

abakɔn
wrist/-a-b-a-k-or-n/

abakɔsɛm
history/-a-b-a-k-or-s-er-m/

aban
government/-a-b-a-n/

abandan
castle/-a-b-a-n-n-a-n/

abandenden
fortress/-a-b-a-n-n-e-n-n-e-n/

abanoma
step-child/-a-b-a-n-o-m-a/

abansoro
storey building/-a-b-a-n-s-o-r-o/

abansoro
upstairs/-a-b-a-n-s-o-r-o/

abantenten

tower/-a-b-a-n-t-e-n-t-e-n/
abanyɛn
adoption/-a-b-a-n-er-n/
abasa
arm/-a-b-a-s-a/
abasirwa
teenager/-a-b-a-s-i-r-w-a/
abasobɔde
award/-a-b-a-s-o-b-or-d-e/
abasode
pledge/-a-b-a-s-o-d-e/
abatow
election/-a-b-a-t-o-w/
abatowmpɔtam
constituency/-a-b-a-t-o-w-m-p-or-t-a-m/
abawoo
childbirth/-a-b-a-w-o-o/
abebɛ
beetle/-a-b-e-b-er/
Abena
Abena/-a-b-e-n-a/
aberante
young man/-a-b-e-r-a-n-t-e/
aberantewa
young boy/-a-b-e-r-a-n-t-e-w-a/
abere a
when/-a-b-e-r-e -a/
aberebiara
always/-a-b-e-r-e-b-i-a-r-a/
aberewa
old lady/-a-b-e-r-e-w-a/
Abesinia

Ethiopia/-a-b-e-s-i-n-i-a/
Abesinianyi
Ethiopian/-a-b-e-s-i-n-i-a-n-i/
abɛ
palm/-a-b-er/
abɛbrɛsɛ
trouble/-a-b-e-r-b-r-e-r-s-e-r/
abɛbusɛm
parable/-a-b-er-b-u-s-er-m/
abɛbɛ
pet/-a-b-er-b-er/
abɛbɛw
grasshopper/-a-b-er-b-er-w/
abɛfua
palmnut/-a-b-er-f-u-a/
abɛn
whistle/-a-b-er-n/
abɛnkwan
palmnut soup/-a-b-er-n-q-a-n/
abɛsɛntrɔw
palmnut wool/-a-b-e-r-s-e-r-n-t-r-o-r-w/
abiasa
three/-a-b-i-a-s-a/
Abibiman Nkabomkuw
African Union/-a-b-i-b-i-m-a-n -n-k-a-b-o-m-k-u-w/
abibir
African/-a-b-i-b-i-r/
Abibir
Africa/a-b-i-b-i-r/
Abibir Anaafo
South Africa/-a-b-i-b-i-r -a-n-a-

a-f-o/
Abibir Anaafonyi
South African/-a-b-i-b-i-r -a-n-
a-a-f-o-n-i-e/
Abibir Finimfin Man
Central African Republic/-a-
b-i-b-i-r -f-i-n-i-m-f-i-n -m-a-n/
Abibir Finimfin Mannyi
Central African/-a-b-i-b-i-r -f-i-
n-i-m-f-i-n -m-a-n-n-i/
abien
two/-a-b-i-e-n/
abirekyi
goat/-a-b-i-r-e-ch-i/
abisaa
riddle/-a-b-i-s-a-a/
aboadabi
locust/-a-b-o-a-d-a-b-i/
aboawa
insect/-a-b-o-a-w-a/
abodoo
bread/-a-b-o-d-o-o/
aboduaba
doll/-a-b-o-d-u-a-b-a/
abofon
nausea/-a-b-o-f-o-n/
abofra
baby/-a-b-o-f-r-a/
abokyi
abochi/-a-b-o-ch-i/
aboloo
cake/-a-b-o-l-o-o/
abomu

sauce/-a-b-o-m-u-o/
abon
bark/-a-b-o-n/
abonsam
devil/-a-b-o-n-s-a-m/
abooboo
wailing/-a-b-o-o-b-o-o/
aboro
sabotage/-a-b-o-r-o/
aborɔba
distinguished/-a-b-o-r-o-r-b-a/
aborɔbɛ
pineapple/-a-b-o-r-o-r-b-e-r/
aborɔdwe
walnut/-a-b-o-r-o-r-d-w-e/
aborɔnoma
dove/-a-b-o-r-o-r-n-o-m-a/
abosomaketew
gecko/-a-b-o-s-o-m-a-k-e-t-e-w/
abosomanketew
chameleon/-a-b-o-s-o-m-a-n-k-e-
t-e-w/
abotare
patience/-a-b-o-t-a-r-e/
abow
door/-a-b-o-w/
abowa
animal/-a-b-o-w-a/
abowano
outdoors/-a-b-o-w-a-n-o/
abowatena
snake/-a-b-o-w-a-t-e-n-a/
abowatia

dwarf/-a-b-o-w-a-t-i-a/
aboyerɛw
heartburn/-a-b-o-y-e-r-e-r-w/
abɔasee
aborigine/-a-b-or-a-s-e-e/
abɔbaado
badge/-a-b-or-b-a-a-d-o/
abɔde
creation/-a-b-or-d-e/
abɔdin
title/-a-b-or-d-i-n/
abɔdinkrataa
certificate/-a-b-o-r-d-i-n-k-r-a-t-a-a/
abɔdo
belt/-a-b-or-d-o/
abɔdwe
chin/-a-b-or-d-w-e/
abɔdwesɛ
beard/-a-b-or-d-w-e-s-er/
abɔndua
axe/-a-b-or-n-n-u-a/
abɔntene
outside/-a-b-or-n-t-e-n-e/
abrabɔ
lifestyle/-a-b-r-a-b-o-r/
abrampa
young/-a-b-r-a-m-p-a/
abrɔba
distinguished/-a-b-r-o-r-b-a/
abrɔme
puzzle/-a-b-r-o-r-m-e/
abufuw

anger/-a-b-u-f-u-w/
abunabun
greenish/-a-b-u-n-a-b-u-n/
aburokyire
abroad/-a-b-u-r-o-ch-i-r-e/
aburow
corn/-a-b-u-r-o-w/
abuwa
pipe/-a-b-u-w-a/
abuwdo
abundant/-a-b-u-w-d-o/
adagye
leisure/-a-d-a-j-e/
adaka
box/-a-d-a-k-a/
adakabɛn
xylophone/-a-d-a-k-a-b-er-n/
adakabɛn
piano/-a-d-a-k-a-b-er-n/
adamfo
friend/-a-d-a-m-f-o/
adanko
hare/-a-d-a-n-k-o/
adanse
proof/-a-d-a-n-s-e/
adante
oyster/-a-d-a-n-t-e/
adar
cutlass/-a-d-a-r/
adare
billhook/-a-d-a-r-e/
adasa
humankind/-a-d-a-s-a/

ade
thing/-a-d-e/
adeaoye
excellence/-a-d-e-a-o-y-e/
adebɔneyɛnyi
evildoer/-a-d-e-b-or-n-e-y-er-n-i/
adedi
inheritance/-a-d-e-d-i/
adehiapaa
priority/-a-d-e-h-i-a-p-a-a/
adehye
royal/-a-d-e-sh-e/
adekoradan
storehouse/-a-d-e-k-o-r-a-d-a-n/
adekyee
daybreak/-a-d-e-ch-e-e/
ademe
ademe/-a-d-e-m-e/
adende
swing/-a-d-e-n-n-e/
adesaa
nightfall/-a-d-e-s-a-a/
adesoa
burden/-a-d-e-s-o-a/
adetɔnni
trader/-a-d-e-t-or-n-n-i/
adeyɛ
skill/-a-d-e-y-er/
adɛn
why/-a-d-er-n/
adiban
food/-a-d-i-b-a-n/
adibanamba

grain/-a-d-i-b-a-n-a-m-m-a/
adidibea
restaurant/-a-d-i-d-i-b-e-a/
adifudi
greed/-a-d-i-f-u-d-i-e/
adigidɔn
cotton/-a-d-i-g-i-d-or-n/
adinkra
symbol/-a-d-i-n-k-r-a/
adiwo
yard/-a-d-i-w-o/
adom
grace/-a-d-o-m/
adow
monkey/-a-d-o-w/
adowa
bee/-a-d-o-w-a/
adɔmba
bell/-a-d-o-r-m-m-a/
adɔntene
advance/-a-d-or-n-t-e-n-e/
adɔpe
ape/-a-d-or-p-e/
adrɛse
address/-a-d-r-e-r-s-e/
aduaba
fruit/-a-d-u-a-b-a/
aduakron
ninety/-a-d-u-a-k-r-o-n/
aduanan
forty/-a-d-u-a-n-a-n/
aduasa
thirty/-a-d-u-a-s-a/

aduasia
 sixty/-a-d-u-a-s-i-a/
aduasuon
 seventy/-a-d-u-a-s-u-o-n/
aduawɔtwe
 eighty/-a-d-u-a-w-or-t-w-e/
aduonu
 twenty/-a-d-u-o-n-u-o/
aduonum
 fifty/-a-d-u-o-n-u-m/
aduru
 drug/-a-d-u-r-u-o/
aduwa
 bean/-a-d-u-w-a/
adwe
 palmkernel/-a-d-w-e/
adwen
 mudfish/-a-d-w-e-n/
adwendwene
 thinking/-a-d-w-e-n-n-w-e-n-e/
adwene
 mind/-a-d-w-e-n-e/
adwenemutew
 intelligent/-a-d-w-e-n-e-m-u-t-e-w/
adwenepɔw
 idea/-a-d-w-e-n-e-p-or-w/
adwengo
 palm kernel oil/-a-d-w-e-n-g-o/
adwenkyerɛ
 thought/-a-d-w-e-n-ch-e-r-e-r/
adwimbea
 workshop/-a-d-w-i-m-m-e-a/

adwin
 technical/-a-d-w-i-n/
adwinsa
 expertise/-a-d-w-i-n-s-a/
Adwoa
 Ajoa/-a-d-w-o-a/
adwuma
 work/-a-d-w-u-m-a/
adwuma
 job/-a-d-w-u-m-a/
adwumabea
 shop/-a-d-w-u-m-a-b-e-a/
adwumakuw
 company/-a-d-w-u-m-a-k-u-w/
adwumapanyin
 boss/-a-d-w-u-m-a-p-a-n-i-n/
adwumatumi
 energy/-a-d-w-u-m-a-t-u-m-i-e/
adwumatumipuw
 radiation/-a-d-w-u-m-a-t-u-m-i-p-u-w/
adwumatɔw
 project/-a-d-w-u-m-a-t-or-w/
adwumawura
 proprietor/-a-d-w-u-m-a-w-u-r-a/
adwumayɛ
 working/-a-d-w-u-m-a-y-er/
ae
 yeah/-a-e/
afa
 side/-a-f-a/
afaban

wall/-a-f-a-b-a-n/
afade
  attire/-a-f-a-d-e/
afahyɛ
  festival/-a-f-a-sh-er/
afanaa
  corners/-a-f-a-n-a-a/
afasew
  water yam/-a-f-a-s-e-w/
afe
  year/-a-f-e/
afe
  comb/-a-f-e/
afeafe
  yearly/-a-f-e-a-f-e/
afebɔɔ
  infinity/-a-f-e-b-or-or/
afebɔɔ
  permanent/-a-f-e-b-or-or/
afeda
  date/-a-f-e-d-a/
afehyia
  whole year/-a-f-e-sh-i-a/
afehyia pa
  happy new year/-a-f-e-sh-i-a -
  p-a/
afei
  now/-a-f-e-i/
afenaa
  slavegirl/-a-f-e-n-a-a/
afɛfɛde
  trinket/-a-f-er-f-er-d-e/
Afganestan

Afghanistan/-a-f-g-a-n-e-s-t-a-n/
Afganestannyi
  Afghan/-a-f-g-a-n-e-s-t-a-n-n-i/
afiri
  machine/-a-f-i-r-i/
afono
  cheek/-a-f-o-n-o/
aforafora
  diverse/-a-f-o-r-a-f-o-r-a/
aforaforadɔm
  diversity/-a-f-o-r-a-f-o-r-a-d-o-r-
  m/
afotu
  advice/-a-f-o-t-u-o/
afɔre
  sacrifice/-a-f-o-r-r-e/
Afrikanse
  Afrikaans/-a-f-r-i-k-a-n-s-e/
Afua
  Efua/-a-f-u-a/
agofa
  act/-a-g-o-f-a/
agofomba
  cast/-a-g-o-f-o-m-m-a/
agoo
  hi/-a-g-o-o/
agoprama
  field/-a-g-o-p-r-a-m-a/
agoro
  game/-a-g-o-r-o/
agoro
  play/-a-g-o-r-o/
agua

chair/-a-g-u-a/
aguabɔ
durbar/-a-g-u-a-b-or/
aguabɛ
guava/-a-g-u-a-b-er/
aguaree
bathroom/-a-g-u-a-r-e-e/
agudi
jewelry/-a-g-u-d-i-e/
agya
dad/-a-j-a/
agyan
bow/-a-j-a-n/
agyapade
property/-a-j-a-p-a-d-e/
agyeei
ouch/-a-j-e-e-i/
agyenkwa
saviour/-a-j-e-n-q-a/
agyinambowa
cat/-a-j-i-n-a-m-m-o-w-a/
agyɛngyɛmbiara
by any chance/-a-j-e-r-n-j-e-r-m-
m-i-a-r-a/
ahaamu
groin/-a-h-a-a-m-u/
ahahan
herb/-a-h-a-h-a-n/
ahahan
salad/-a-h-a-h-a-n/
ahanamakye
dawn/-a-h-a-n-a-m-a-c-h-e/
Ahanamanta

harmattan/-a-h-a-n-a-m-a-n-t-a/
ahantan
pride/-a-h-a-n-t-a-n/
ahemfie
palace/-a-h-e-m-f-i-e/
ahen
how much/-a-h-e-n/
ahenegua
throne/-a-h-e-n-e-g-u-a/
ahenekurow
capital/-a-h-e-n-e-k-u-r-o-w/
ahenekyɛw
crown/-a-h-e-n-e-c-h-er-w/
aheneman
kingdom/-a-h-e-n-e-m-a-n/
ahenewa
nobility/-a-h-e-n-e-w-a/
ahi
annoying/-a-h-i/
ahiade
demand/-a-h-i-a-d-e/
ahihunu
prejudice/-a-h-i-h-u-n-u-o/
Ahinime
October/a-h-i-n-i-m-e/
ahintasɛmfua
password/-a-h-i-n-t-a-s-er-m-f-u-
a/
ahisɛm
annoyance/-a-h-i-s-er-m/
ahobambɔ
security/-a-h-o-b-a-m-m-or/
ahoboa

preparation/-a-h-o-b-o-a/
ahoboaboa
preparations/-a-h-o-b-o-a-b-o-a/
ahobow
surprise/-a-h-o-b-o-w/
ahobrɛase
humility/-a-h-o-b-r-e-r-a-s-e/
ahobrɛase
humble/-a-h-o-b-r-e-r-a-s-e/
ahodow
different/-a-h-o-d-o-w/
ahofadi
liberty/-a-h-o-f-a-d-i/
ahokyere
hardship/-a-h-o-c-h-e-r-e/
ahoma
string/-a-h-o-m-a/
ahome
breath/-a-h-o-m-e/
ahomeka
comfort/-a-h-o-m-e-k-a/
ahometew
distress/-a-h-o-m-e-t-e-w/
ahonde
bead/-a-h-o-n-n-e/
ahonya
wealth/-a-h-o-n-y-a/
ahonyade
asset/-a-h-o-n-y-a-d-e/
ahonyaguatiri
infrastructure/-a-h-o-n-y-a-g-u-a-t-i-r-i/
ahopopo

trembling/-a-h-o-p-o-p-o/
ahoroba
insult/-a-h-o-r-o-b-a/
ahorobahyehyɛ
diss/-a-h-o-r-o-b-a-sh-e-sh-e-r/
ahorobahyɛ
insults/-a-h-o-r-o-b-a-sh-e-r/
ahorow
several/-a-h-o-r-o-w/
ahosu
color/-a-h-o-s-u-o/
ahotoso
trust/-a-h-o-t-o-s-o/
ahotɔ
luxury/-a-h-o-t-or/
ahoɔden
strength/-a-h-o-or-d-e-n/
ahoɔfɛw
beauty/-a-h-o-or-f-er-w/
ahoɔyaa
envy/-a-h-o-or-y-a-a/
ahɔhodan
guest room/-a-h-or-h-o-d-a-n/
ahɔhofi
hotel/-a-h-or-h-o-f-i-e/
ahɔre
phlegm/-a-h-o-r-r-e/
ahuhurobere
summer/-a-h-u-h-u-r-o-b-e-r-e/
ahum
storm/-a-h-u-m/
ahumbɔbɔ
mercy/-a-h-u-m-m-or-b-or/

ahunabɔbirim
awesome/-a-h-u-n-a-b-o-r-b-i-r-i-m/
ahuon
brain/-a-h-u-o-n/
ahuon-ntini
nerve/-a-h-u-o-n-n-t-i-n-i/
ahwede
sugarcane/-a-h-w-e-d-e/
ahwehwɛ
mirror/-a-h-w-e-h-w-er/
ahwehwɛanyiwa
spectacles/-a-h-w-e-h-w-er-a-n-i-w-a/
ahwɛyie
carefulness/-a-h-w-er-y-i-e/
ahwɛyiemu
carefully/-a-h-w-er-y-i-e-m-u/
ahyeawo
prostitute/-a-sh-e-a-w-o/
Ahyia
Asia/-a-sh-i-a/
ahyiadi
conference/-a-sh-i-a-d-i/
ahyɛase
beginning/-a-sh-er-a-s-e/
ahyɛmu
testament/-a-sh-er-m-u/
ahyɛnsew
sign/-a-sh-er-n-s-e-w/
akado
paint/-a-k-a-d-o/
akam

Mark/-a-k-a-m/
Akan
Akan/-a-k-a-n/
akaniakaba
philanderer/-a-s-a-n-t-e -t-w-i-i-a-k-a-b-a/
akansi
competition/-a-s-a-n-t-e -t-w-i-s-i/
akansi-agodi
sport/-a-s-a-n-t-e -t-w-i-s-i-a-g-o-d-i-e/
akasa
cymbal/-a-k-a-s-a/
akasakasa
friction/-a-k-a-s-a-k-a-s-a/
akatawia
umbrella/-a-k-a-t-a-w-i-a/
akate
capsid/-a-k-a-t-e/
akatewa
melon seed/-a-k-a-t-e-w-a/
akatua
compensation/-a-k-a-t-u-a/
akenkan
reading/-a-k-e-n-k-a-n/
akentengua
stool/-a-k-e-n-t-e-n-g-u-a/
ako
war/-a-k-o/
akoangoa
yellow/-a-k-o-a-n-g-o-a/
akobɛn

warhorn/-a-k-o-b-er-n/
akode
weapon/-a-k-o-d-e/
akoko
chest/-a-k-o-k-o/
akokoduru
courage/-a-k-o-k-o-d-u-r-u-o/
akokora
old man/-a-k-o-k-o-r-a/
akokɔ
chicken/-a-k-o-k-or/
akokɔbirisɛm
aggression/-a-k-o-k-o-r-b-i-r-i-s-e-r-m/
akokɔnyin
cockerel/-a-k-o-k-or-n-i-n/
akokɔre
diarrhoea/-a-k-o-k-o-r-r-e/
akoma
heart/-a-k-o-m-a/
akomaden
stamina/-a-k-o-m-a-d-e-n/
akomantini
artery/-a-k-o-m-a-n-t-i-n-i/
akonkoran
crow/-a-k-o-n-k-o-r-a-n/
akoo
parrot/-a-k-o-o/
akora
preservation/-a-k-o-r-a/
akorade
treasure/-a-k-o-r-a-d-e/
akotene

main/-a-k-o-t-e-n-e/
akowa
servant/-a-k-o-w-a/
akɔaba
welcome/-a-k-or-a-b-a/
akɔmfɛm
guinea-fowl/-a-k-or-m-f-er-m/
akɔndɔ
desirable/-a-k-or-n-n-or/
akɔndɔakɔndɔ
very desirable/-a-k-or-n-n-or-a-k-or-n-n-or/
akɔneaba
to-and-fro/-a-k-or-n-e-a-b-a/
akɔnsɔn
baboon/-a-k-or-n-s-or-n/
akrante
hedgehog/-a-k-r-a-n-t-e/
akron
nine/-a-k-r-o-n/
akrɔma
hawk/-a-k-r-o-r-m-a/
Aktek
Arctic/a-k-t-e-k/
Akua
Ekua/-a-k-u-a/
Akuapem
Akuapem/-a-k-u-a-p-e-m/
akuraa
community/-a-k-u-r-a-a/
akuraase
village/-a-k-u-r-a-a-s-e/
akutu

orange/-a-k-u-t-u-o/
akwadaa
toddler/-a-q-a-d-a-a/
akwadwere
apathy/-a-q-a-d-w-e-r-e/
akwahosan
health/-a-q-a-h-o-s-a-n/
akwambew
problem/-a-q-a-m-m-e-w/
akwanhyia
accident/-a-q-a-n-sh-i-a/
akwanma
vacation/-a-q-a-n-m-a/
akwantu
exploration/-a-q-a-n-t-u/
akwantu
journey/-a-q-a-n-t-u/
akwantunhyehyɛe
transportation/-a-q-a-n-t-u-n-sh-e-sh-er-e/
akyekyenduru
preservative/-a-ch-e-ch-e-n-n-u-r-u-o/
akyekyerɛ
tortoise/-a-ch-e-ch-e-r-e-r/
akyem
weaverbird/-a-ch-e-m/
akyemfowa
swallow/-a-ch-e-m-f-o-w-a/
akyere
ugly/-a-ch-e-r-e/
akyerɛbaa
sister/-a-ch-e-r-e-r-b-a-a/

akyerɛwamba
alphabet/-a-ch-e-r-e-r-w-a-m-m-a/
akyi
behind/-a-ch-i/
akyingye
doubt/-a-ch-i-n-j-e/
akyiri
back/-a-ch-i-r-i/
akyiriyi
later/-a-ch-i-r-i-y-i/
akyiwade
abomination/-a-ch-i-w-a-d-e/
akyɛde
gift/-a-ch-er-d-e/
alaagyi
alhaji/-a-l-a-a-j-i/
Alata
Nigeria/-a-l-a-t-a/
Alatanyi
Nigerian/-a-l-a-t-a-n-i/
aleluya
hallelujah/-a-l-e-l-u-y-a/
alɛgyi
allergy/-a-l-er-j-i/
alɛgyiki
allergic/-a-l-er-j-i-k-i/
algoredeme
algorithm/-a-l-g-o-r-e-d-e-m-e/
alikɔpta
helicopter/-a-l-i-k-or-p-t-a/
aluminiyɔm
aluminium/-a-l-u-m-i-n-i-y-or-m/

amade
supply/-a-m-a-d-e/
amambere
culture/-a-m-a-m-m-e-r-e/
amambrɛ
tradition/-a-m-a-m-m-r-e-r/
amambu
governance/-a-m-a-m-m-u/
amambɔe
treason/-a-m-a-m-m-or-e/
amamfi
giant/-a-m-a-m-f-i/
amamforanyi
refugee/-a-m-a-m-f-o-r-a-n-i/
amande
custom/-a-m-a-n-n-e/
amandehu
suffering/-a-m-a-n-n-e-h-u/
amandeɛ
report/-a-m-a-n-n-e-er/
amandeɛbɔ
announcement/-a-m-a-n-n-e-er-b-or/
amandɔ
patriotism/-a-m-a-n-n-or/
amanko
civil war/-a-m-a-n-k-o/
amansuon
realm/-a-m-a-n-s-u-o-n/
amanyɛ
politics/-a-m-a-n-er/
amanyɛkuw
political party/-a-m-a-n-er-k-u-

w/
amanyɛnyi
politician/-a-m-a-n-er-n-i/
Amarinya
Amharic/-a-m-a-r-i-n-y-a/
Amba
Ama/-a-m-m-a/
amba
seed/-a-m-m-a/
amba
dice/-a-m-m-a/
ambaade
armpit/-a-m-m-a-a-d-e/
ambatow
voting/-a-m-m-a-t-o-w/
ambrado
governor/-a-m-m-r-a-d-o/
ambɛn
horn/-a-m-m-er-n/
amen
amen/-a-m-e-n/
Amɛreka
America/-a-m-e-r-r-e-k-a/
Amɛreka Amankuw
United States of America/-a-m-e-r-r-e-k-a -a-m-a-n-k-u-w/
Amɛrekanyi
American/-a-m-e-r-r-e-k-a-n-i/
Aminia
Armenia/-a-m-i-n-i-a/
Aminianyi
Armenian/-a-m-i-n-i-a-n-i/
amokua

squirrel/-a-m-o-k-u-a/
amonade
delivery/-a-m-o-n-a-d-e/
ampa
true/-a-m-p-a/
ampaara
truly/-a-m-p-a-a-r-a/
ampe
ampay/-a-m-p-e/
amudɔ
deep/-a-m-u-d-or/
ana
before/-a-n-a/
anaa
or/-a-n-a-a/
anaafo
south/-a-n-a-a-f-o/
Anaafo Koria
South Korea/-a-n-a-a-f-o k-o-r-i-a/
Anaafo Korianyi
South Korean/-a-n-a-a-f-o k-o-r-i-a-n-i/
anadwe
night/-a-n-a-d-w-e/
anamuna
watermelon/-a-n-a-m-u-n-a/
anamɔnkwan
path/-a-n-a-m-or-n-q-a-n/
anan
four/-a-n-a-n/
ananade
sole/-a-n-a-n-a-d-e/

ananse
spider/-a-n-a-n-s-e/
anansesɛm
story/-a-n-a-n-s-e-s-er-m/
ananta
bow-legged/-a-n-a-n-t-a/
anapa
morning/-a-n-a-p-a/
anapaduan
breakfast/-a-n-a-p-a-d-u-a-n/
anee
west/-a-n-e-e/
anenamfikyiri
homeless/-a-n-e-n-a-m-f-i-ch-i-r-i/
angoa
vegetable oil/-a-n-g-o-a/
Angola
Angola/-a-n-g-o-l-a/
Angolanyi
Angolan/-a-n-g-o-l-a-n-i/
anhwea
sand/-a-n-h-w-e-a/
ankama
lime/-a-n-k-a-m-a/
ankasa
real/-a-n-k-a-s-a/
ankora
barrel/-a-n-k-o-r-a/
ankɔbea
steward/-a-n-k-or-b-e-a/
annkadaade
swift/-a-n-n-k-a-d-a-a-d-e/

annworogyeraase
mammy-truck/-a-n-n-w-o-r-o-j-e-r-a-a-s-e/

ano
mouth/-a-n-o/

anoaduru
solution/-a-n-o-a-d-u-r-u-o/

anobam
lipbalm/-a-n-o-b-a-m/

anofamfa
lip/-a-n-o-f-a-m-f-a/

anohoba
promise/-a-n-o-h-o-b-a/

anokum
gossip/-a-n-o-k-u-m/

anoma
bird/-a-n-o-m-a/

anowatar
perfume/-a-n-o-w-a-t-a-r/

Antaateka
Antartica/-a-n-t-a-a-t-e-k-a/

ante
aunt/-a-n-t-e/

antuhu
towel/-a-n-t-u-h-u-o/

anu
both/-a-n-u/

anuho
remorse/-a-n-u-h-o/

anum
five/-a-n-u-m/

anuma
baptism/-a-n-u-m-a/

anwensɛm
poem/-a-n-w-e-n-s-er-m/

anwew
onion/-a-n-w-e-w/

anwewba
chives/-a-n-w-e-w-b-a/

anyi
eye/-a-n-i/

anyi sɔ
appreciate/-a-n-i -s-or/

anyiannsɔ
unappreciativeness/-a-n-i-a-n-n-s-or/

anyibere
covetuousness/-a-n-i-b-e-r-e/

anyibere
serious/-a-n-i-b-e-r-e/

anyibuei
worldliness/-a-n-i-b-u-e-i/

anyidado
hope/-a-n-i-d-a-d-o/

anyidi
respect/-a-n-i-d-i/

anyidi
dignifying/-n-i-d-i/

anyidifata
dignity/-a-n-i-d-i-f-a-t-a/

anyiduado
lapse/-a-n-i-d-u-a-d-o/

anyifura
blindness/-a-n-i-f-u-r-a/

anyigye
joy/-a-n-i-j-e/

anyigye
 happiness/-a-n-i-j-e/
anyigye-anyigye
 happy/-a-n-i-j-e-a-n-i-j-e/
anyihaw
 laziness/-a-n-i-h-a-w/
anyika
 entertaining/-a-n-i-k-a/
anyikom
 drowsiness/-a-n-i-k-o-m/
anyikom
 sleepiness/-a-n-i-k-o-m/
anyikosua
 eyeball/-a-n-i-k-o-s-u-a/
anyimguase
 disgrace/-a-n-i-m-g-u-a-s-e/
anyimpa
 favor/-a-n-i-m-p-a/
anyimpi
 force/-a-n-i-m-p-i/
anyimtia
 contempt/-a-n-i-m-t-i-a/
anyimu
 face/-a-n-i-m-u/
anyimu
 in front/-a-n-i-m-u/
anyimu
 front/-a-n-i-m-u/
anyimunyam
 glory/-a-n-i-m-u-n-y-a-m/
anyina
 silk cotton tree/-a-n-i-n-a/
anyinam

 electricity/-a-n-i-n-a-m/
anyinam
 lightning/-a-n-i-n-a-m/
anyinamde
 electric/-a-n-i-n-a-m-d-e/
anyinsu
 tear/-a-n-i-n-s-u/
anyinsuwa
 teardrop/-a-n-i-n-s-u-w-a/
anyintɔn
 eyebrow/-a-n-i-n-t-or-n/
anyisoatɛw
 eyelash/-a-n-i-s-o-a-t-er-w/
anyisɔ
 pleasure/-a-n-i-s-or/
anyitan
 enmity/-a-n-i-t-a-n/
anyito
 shame/-a-n-i-t-o/
anyiwaden
 determination/-a-n-i-w-a-d-e-n/
anyiwamba
 pupil/-a-n-i-w-a-m-m-a/
anyiwaseatew
 clever/-a-n-i-w-a-s-e-a-t-e-w/
anyɛn
 genius/-a-n-er-n/
anyɛn
 witchcraft/-a-n-er-n/
anyɛn-banyin
 wizard/-a-n-er-n-b-a-n-i-n/
anyɛn-basia
 witch/-a-n-er-n-b-a-s-i-a/

anyɛnkoyɛ
friendship/-a-n-er-n-k-o-y-er/

ao
oh/-a-o/

apa
framework/-a-p-a/

apaam
plan/-a-p-a-a-m/

apakan
hammock/-a-p-a-s-a-n-t-e -t-w-i/

apam
covenant/-a-p-a-m/

apampa
tray/-a-p-a-m-p-a/

apaso
scissors/-a-p-a-s-o/

apem
thousand/-a-p-e-m/

aper
apple/-a-p-e-r/

apɛde
desire/-a-p-er-d-e/

aplekehyɛn
application/-a-p-l-e-k-e-sh-er-n/

apolo
conjunctivitis/-a-p-o-l-o/

apɔtɔbibiri
mud/-a-p-o-r-t-o-r-b-i-b-i-r-i/

aprandaa
thunder/-a-p-r-a-n-n-a-a/

apuei
sunrise/-a-p-u-e-i/

ara
just/-a-r-a/

aroplen
plane/-a-r-o-p-l-e-n/

as☐de
duty/-a-s -d-e/

asaase
earth/-a-s-a-a-s-e/

asaase
land/-a-s-a-a-s-e/

asaasetaw
continent/-a-s-a-a-s-e-t-a-w/

asaasewosow
earthquake/-a-s-a-a-s-e-w-o-s-o-w/

asado
living-room/-a-s-a-d-o/

asafo
warriors/-a-s-a-f-o/

asam
pigeon/-a-s-a-m/

asare
hall/-a-s-a-r-e/

asatiri
ransom/-a-s-a-t-i-r-i/

asaw
dancing/-a-s-a-w/

asawu
net/-a-s-a-w-u/

asawwura
dustpan/-a-s-a-w-w-u-r-a/

ase
down/-a-s-e/

ase
 under/-a-s-e/
ase
 under/-a-s-e/
aseda
 thanks/-a-s-e-d-a/
asen
 loin/-a-s-e-n/
asenade
 downstairs/-a-s-e-n-a-d-e/
asera
 snuff/-a-s-e-r-a/
aserewsɛm
 joke/-a-s-e-r-e-w-s-e-r-m/
asesawnsu
 pail/-a-s-e-s-a-w-n-s-u/
asetaagyee
 sock/-a-s-e-t-a-a-j-e-e/
asew
 inlaw/-a-s-e-w/
asɛde
 responsibility/-a-s-er-d-e/
asɛm
 issue/-a-s-er-m/
asɛmbisa
 question/-a-s-er-m-m-i-s-a/
asɛmpa
 gospel/-a-s-er-m-p-a/
asɛmpakanyi
 preacher/-a-s-er-m-p-a-s-a-n-t-e
 -t-w-i-y-i/
asɛmpatrɛwnyi
 missionary/-a-s-e-r-m-p-a-t-r-e-

r-w-n-i/
asɛmpɔw
 heading/-a-s-er-m-p-or-w/
asɛndii
 judgement/-a-s-er-n-n-i-i/
asɛndiibea
 court/-a-s-er-n-n-i-i-b-e-a/
asɛndiinyi
 judge/-a-s-er-n-n-i-i-n-i/
Asi
 Esi/a-s-i/
asia
 six/-a-s-i-a/
asiam
 flour/-a-s-i-a-m/
asiane
 misfortune/-a-s-i-a-n-e/
asiesɛm
 secret/-a-s-i-e-s-er-m/
asikyire
 sugar/-a-s-i-ch-i-r-e/
asikyireamba
 raisin/-a-s-i-ch-i-r-e-a-m-m-a/
asoaso
 donkey/-a-s-o-a-s-o/
asoasoa
 rabbit/-a-s-o-a-s-o-a/
asomafo
 messengers/-a-s-o-m-a-f-o/
asombɛn
 ivory/-a-s-o-m-m-er-n/
Asombɛn Mpoano
 Cote d'Ivoire/-a-s-o-m-m-er-n -

m-p-o-a-n-o/
Asombɛn Mpoanonyi
Ivoirian/-a-s-o-m-m-er-n-m-p-o-
a-n-o-n-i-e/
asomuade
earpiece/-a-s-o-m-u-a-d-e/
asomudwoe
peace/-a-s-o-m-u-d-w-o-e/
asopatere
shoe/-a-s-o-p-a-t-e-r-e/
asorɛkye
wave/-a-s-o-r-e-r-ch-e/
asotie
obedience/-a-s-o-t-i-e/
asowa
ear/-a-s-o-w-a/
asowamuade
earring/-a-s-o-w-a-m-u-a-d-e/
asoɛe
lodge/-a-s-o-er-e/
asɔre
church/-a-s-o-r-r-e/
asɔredan
temple/-a-s-o-r-r-e-d-a-n/
asɔw
hoe/-a-s-or-w/
asuba
stream/-a-s-u-b-a/
asuom
wee hours/-a-s-u-o-m/
asuon
seven/-a-s-u-o-n/
Asusow

wet season/a-s-u-s-o-w/
Asusow Aketeaba
May/-a-s-u-s-o-w-a-k-e-t-e-a-b-a/
ata
twin/-a-t-a/
ataade
garment/-a-t-a-a-d-e/
atadwe
tigernut/-a-t-a-d-w-e/
atare
dress/-a-t-a-r-e/
ateetee
oppression/-a-t-e-e-t-e-e/
atenka
feeling/-a-t-e-n-k-a/
atere
spoon/-a-t-e-r-e/
atɛntenenee
justice/-a-t-er-n-t-e-n-e-n-e-e/
atɛntɛbɛn
flute/-a-t-er-n-t-er-b-er-n/
atibɛn
catarrh/-a-t-i-b-er-n/
atifi
north/-a-t-i-f-i/
atifi
summit/-a-t-i-f-i/
Atifi Koria
North Korea/-a-t-i-f-i k-o-r-i-a/
Atifi Korianyi
North Korean/-a-t-i-f-i k-o-r-i-a-
n-i/
atikɔ

back of the head/-a-t-i-k-or/
atiridii
 fever/-a-t-i-r-i-d-i-i/
Atlantek
 Atlantic/-a-t-l-a-n-t-e-k/
atliti
 athlete/-a-t-l-i-t-i/
atoko
 millet/-a-t-o-k-o/
atombo
 anvil/-a-t-o-m-m-o/
atoro
 lie/-a-t-o-r-o/
atɔe
 sunset/-a-t-or-e/
atɔm
 atom/-a-t-or-m/
atuduru
 gunpowder/-a-t-u-d-u-r-u-o/
atumpan
 talking drum/-a-t-u-m-p-a-n/
atuu
 hug/-a-t-u-u/
atwede
 stair/-a-t-w-e-d-e/
atwere
 ladder/-a-t-w-e-r-e/
atwetwe
 scorn/-a-t-w-e-t-w-e/
atwɛre
 quarrel/-a-t-w-e-r-r-e/
atwɛre
 frog/-a-t-w-e-r-r-e/

aware
 marriage/-a-w-a-r-e/
awaregu
 divorce/-a-w-a-r-e-g-u/
awendade
 lion/-a-w-e-n-n-a-d-e/
awengaa
 pedophile/-a-w-e-n-g-a-a/
awerɛfiri
 forgetfulness/-a-w-e-r-e-r-f-i-r-i/
awerɛfirimu
 suddenly/-a-w-e-r-e-r-f-i-r-i-m-u/
awerɛhow
 grief/-a-w-e-r-e-r-h-o-w/
awerɛhow
 sadness/-a-w-e-r-e-r-h-o-w/
awerɛhyɛmu
 confidence/-a-w-e-r-e-r-sh-e-r-m-u/
awerɛkyekyer
 consolation/-a-w-e-r-e-r-ch-e-ch-e-r/
awerɛw
 nail/-a-w-e-r-e-r-w/
awi
 thief/-a-w-i/
awia
 sun/-a-w-i-a/
awiaawia
 sunny/-a-w-i-a-a-w-i-a/
awiabere
 afternoon/-a-w-i-a-b-e-r-e/

awiei
end/-a-w-i-e-i/
awiei
behind/-a-w-i-e-i/
awifua
wheat/-a-w-i-f-u-a/
awimbere
evening/-a-w-i-m-m-e-r-e/
awoda
birthday/-a-w-o-d-a/
awode
womb/-a-w-o-d-e/
awofo
parents/-a-w-o-f-o/
awoo
birth/-a-w-o-o/
awɔse
goosebumps/-a-w-or-s-e/
awɔtwe
eight/-a-w-or-t-w-e/
awɔw
freezing/-a-w-or-w/
awɔwbere
winter/-a-w-o-r-w-b-e-r-e/
awudi
murder/-a-w-u-d-i-e/
awur
padlock/-a-w-u-r/
awura
lady/-a-w-u-r-a/
awuraa
miss/-a-w-u-r-a-a/
awuraba
mistress/-a-w-u-r-a-b-a/
Awurade
Lord/-a-w-u-r-a-d-e/
ayamuhyehye
compassion/-a-y-a-m-u-sh-e-sh-e/
ayamuyie
generosity/-a-y-a-m-u-y-i-e/
ayamuyie
kindness/-a-y-a-m-u-y-i-e/
ayamuɔwen
stinginess/-a-y-a-m-u-or-w-e-n/
ayaresabea
clinic/-a-y-a-r-e-s-a-b-e-a/
ayeforo
bride/-a-y-e-f-o-r-o/
ayeforohyia
wedding/-a-y-e-f-o-r-o-sh-i-a/
ayeforokunu
bridegroom/-a-y-e-f-o-r-o-k-u-n-u-o/
ayekoo
well done/-a-y-e-k-o-o/
ayerfa
adultery/-a-y-e-r-f-a/
ayɛnkoyɛnko
friendly/-a-y-er-n-k-o-y-er-n-k-o/
ayɛw
praise/-a-y-er-w/
Ayɛwoho
July/-a-y-er-w-o-h-o/
Ayɛwohomumu
June/-a-y-er-w-o-h-o-m-u-m-u-o/

ayɛyi
adulation/-a-y-er-y-i/
ayi
funeral/-a-y-i/
ayodiin
iodine/-a-y-o-d-i-i-n/
ayowa
bowl/-a-y-o-w-a/
ayoyo
ayoyo/-a-y-o-y-o/
azaa
rascal/-az-a-a/
Azɛbaegyan
Azerbaijan/-az-er-b-a-e-j-a-n/
Azɛbaegyannyi
Azerbaijani/-az-er-b-a-e-j-a-n-n-i/
azonto
azonto/-az-o-n-t-o/
b
b/-b/
ba
come/-b-a/
ba
child/-b-a/
baa
woman/-b-a-a/
baa … mu
loosen/-b-a-a … -m-u/
baabi
somewhere/-b-a-a-b-i/
baage
bag/-b-a-a-g-e/

baako
one person/-b-a-a-k-o/
baakron
nine persons/-b-a-a-k-r-o-n/
baanan
four persons/-f-o -a-n-a-n/
baanu
two persons/-b-a-a-n-u/
baanum
five persons/-b-a-a-n-u-m/
baasa
three persons/-b-a-a-s-a/
baasakoro
trinity/-b-a-a-s-a-k-o-r-o/
baasia
six persons/-b-a-a-s-i-a/
baasuon
seven persons/-b-a-a-s-u-o-n/
baatan
female parent/-b-a-a-t-a-n -b-e-a/
baatan
parent/-b-a-a-t-a-n/
baawɔtwe
eight persons/-b-a-a-w-or-t-w-e/
baba
memorize/-b-a-b-a/
babadi
memorization/-b-a-b-a-d-i/
babanyin
son/-b-a-b-a-n-i-n/
babasia
daughter/-b-a-b-a-s-i-a/

babiree
plenty/-b-a-b-i-r-e-e/
badwoa
ovary/-b-a-d-w-o-a/
bae
extend/-b-a-e/
baebae
fare well/-b-a-e-b-a-e/
baebol
bible/-b-a-e-b-o-l/
baesekel
bicycle/-b-a-e-s-e-k-e-l/
bafa
cubit/-b-a-f-a/
bafua
singleton/-b-a-f-u-a/
bafuu
rich/-b-a-f-u-u/
bagua
public/-b-a-g-u-a/
baguanyi
councillor/-b-a-g-u-a-n-i/
bahaw
fatigue/-b-a-h-a-w/
baka
lagoon/-b-a-k-a/
balun
balloon/-b-a-l-u-n/
bamba
ledge/-b-a-m-m-a/
bambɔ
protection/-b-a-m-m-or/
ban

fence/-b-a-n/
banana
grandchild/-b-a-n-a-n-a/
Bangladɛhye
Bangladesh/b-a-n-g-l-a-d-er-sh-e/
Bangladɛhyenyi
Bangladeshi/b-a-n-g-l-a-d-er-sh-e-n-i/
banke
bank/-b-a-n-k-e/
banku
banku/-b-a-n-k-u/
bankum
left/-b-a-n-k-u-m/
bankye
cassava/-b-a-n-ch-e/
banyimba
boy/-b-a-n-i-m-m-a/
banyin
man/-b-a-n-i-n/
bara
forbid/-b-a-r-a/
Baren
Bahrain/b-a-r-e-n/
Barennyi
Bahraini/b-a-r-e-n-n-i/
barima
male/-b-a-r-i-m-a/
basaa
distressed/-b-a-s-a-a/
basabasa
unkempt/-b-a-s-a-b-a-s-a/

basia
 female/-b-a-s-i-a/
basiaba
 girl/-b-a-s-i-a-b-a/
basiaba
 damsel/-b-a-s-i-a-b-a/
basiaba
 such as this/-b-a-s-i-a-b-a/
bata
 trade/-b-a-t-a/
batadi
 trading/-b-a-t-a-d-i/
batakeri
 robe/-b-a-t-a-k-e-r-i/
batanyi
 customer/-b-a-t-a-n-i/
baten
 button/-b-a-t-e-n/
batiri
 shoulder/-b-a-t-i-r-i/
batri
 battery/-b-a-t-r-i/
batwɛre
 elbow/-b-a-t-w-e-r-r-e/
bayere
 yam/-b-a-y-e-r-e/
bayi
 sorcery/-b-a-y-i/
bayolɔgyi
 biology/-b-a-y-o-l-or-j-i/
bea
 place/-b-e-a/
bea

 female/-b-e-a/
beabiara
 everywhere/-b-e-a-b-i-a-r-a/
befo
 mourner/-b-e-f-o/
ben
 prepare/-b-e-n/
Benada
 Tuesday/b-e-n-a-d-a/
bene
 be cooked/-b-e-n-e/
bepɔw
 mountain/-b-e-p-or-w/
ber
 surf/-b-e-r/
berano
 harbour/-b-e-r-a-n-o/
berdum
 purple/-b-e-r-d-u-m/
bere
 moment/-b-e-r-e/
bere
 ripen/-b-e-r-e/
bere
 fertile/-b-e-r-e/
beree
 sexy/-b-e-r-e-e/
bereku
 eel/-b-e-r-e-k-u/
beriliyɔm
 beryllium/-b-e-r-i-l-i-y-o-r-m/
bese
 kola nut/-b-e-s-e/

bese
 kolanut/-b-e-s-e/
bɛ
 proverb/-b-er/
bɛɛsen
 basin/-b-er-er-s-e-n/
bɛhwɛadenyi
 spectator/-b-er-h-w-er-a-d-e-n-i/
bɛlɛ
 dimwit/-b-er-l-er/
bɛn
 near/-b-er-n/
bɛn
 approach/-b-er-n/
bɛn
 arrow/-b-er-n/
bɛn
 which/-b-er-n/
Bɛnin
 Benin/b-er-n-i-n/
Bɛninnyi
 Beninois/b-er-n-i-n-n-i/
bɛnkye
 bench/-b-er-n-ch-e/
bɛntoa
 syringe/-b-er-n-t-o-a/
bɛr
 mattress/-b-e-r-r/
bi
 some/-b-i/
bi
 some/-b-i/
bi ka ho

 more/-b-i -k-a -h-o/
biara
 each/-b-i-a-r-a/
biara
 every/-b-i-a-r-a/
biara
 any/-b-i-a-r-a/
bibir
 African/-b-i-b-i-r/
biew
 bone/-b-i-e-w/
biɛɛ
 beer/-b-i-er-er/
bin
 dung/-b-i-n/
biom
 again/-b-i-o-m/
biom-so
 more/-b-i-o-m-s-o/
bireku
 woodpigeon/-b-i-r-e-k-u/
birekutu
 scarecrow/-b-i-r-e-k-u-t-u-o/
biribi
 something/-b-i-r-i-b-i/
biribi
 something/-b-i-r-i-b-i/
biribiara
 everything/-b-i-r-i-b-i-a-r-a/
birim
 bruise/-b-i-r-i-m/
biriw
 charcoal/-b-i-r-i-w/

bisa
ask/-b-i-s-a/
bisade
request/-b-i-s-a-d-e/
bisafo
requester/-b-i-s-a-f-o/
Bisaw-Gini
Guinea-Bissau/b-i-s-a-w-g-i-n-i/
Bisaw-Gininyi
Bissau-Guinean/b-i-s-a-w-g-i-n-i-n-i/
bisibisibasaa
confusion/-b-i-s-i-b-i-s-i-b-a-s-a-a/
biso
other/-b-i-s-o/
blɔge
blog/-b-l-or-g-e/
bo
price/-b-o/
boa
help/-b-o-a/
boaboa
gather/-b-o-a-b-o-a/
boafo
assistant/-b-o-a-f-o/
boafo
helper/-b-o-a-f-o/
boba
stone/-b-o-b-a/
bobe
vine/-b-o-b-e/
bobe nsa

wine/-b-o-b-e -n-s-a/
bobeaba
grape/-b-o-b-e-a-b-a/
bobɔw
fold/-b-o-b-or-w/
bofrot
dumpling/-b-o-f-r-o-t/
boka
east/-b-o-k-a/
Boka Timɔ
East Timor/b-o-k-a t-i-m-or/
Boka Timɔnyi
East Timorese/b-o-k-a t-i-m-or-n-i/
bokiti
bucket/-b-o-k-i-t-i/
bomu
join/-b-o-m-u-o/
bon
shell/-b-o-n/
bon
scale/-b-o-n/
bonso
whale/-b-o-n-s-o/
bonyiayɛ
ungrateful/-b-o-n-i-a-y-er/
boonyi
ambassador/-b-o-o-n-i-e/
boro
swim/-b-o-r-o/
boro
beat/-b-o-r-o/
borɔfo

English/-b-o-r-o-r-f-o/
borɔn
boron/-b-o-r-o-r-n/
borɔsow
brush/-b-o-r-o-r-s-o-w/
borɛde
plantain/-b-o-r-e-r-d-e/
bosea
loan/-b-o-s-e-a/
bosom
fetish/-b-o-s-o-m/
bosompo
ocean/-b-o-s-o-m-p-o/
bosoome
month/-b-o-s-o-o-m-e/
bosoome
moon/-b-o-s-o-o-m-e/
bota
vaccinate/-b-o-t-a/
botae
aim/-b-o-t-a-e/
botan
rock/-b-o-t-a-n/
bow
be drunk/-b-o-w/
bowa
be wrong/-b-o-w-a/
bɔ
mention/-b-or/
bɔ
create/-b-or/
bɔ
hit/-b-or/

bɔ ... aboro
sabotage/-b-o-r ... -a-b-o-r-o/
bɔ ... anohoba
promise/-b-or ... -a-n-o-h-o-b-a/
bɔ ... asowa mu
slap/-b-or ... -a-s-o-w-a -m-u/
bɔ ... asu
baptise/-b-or ... -a-s-u/
bɔ ... bosea
loan/-b-or ... -b-o-s-e-a/
bɔ ... dua
curse/-b-or ... -d-u-a/
bɔ ... ho ban
protect/-b-or ... -h-o -b-a-n/
bɔ ... ho dawuru
advertise/-b-o-r ... -h-o -d-a-w-u-r-u-o/
bɔ ... krɔnoo
burgle/-b-o-r ... -k-r-o-r-n-o-o/
bɔ ... kɔkɔ
warn/-b-or ... -k-or-k-or/
bɔ ... mbɔden
strive/-b-or ... -m-m-or-d-e-n/
bɔ ... nkae
remind/-b-or ... -n-k-a-e/
bɔ ... patapaa
bully/-b-or ... -p-a-t-a-p-a-a/
bɔ ... somebo
accuse/-b-or ... -s-o-m-e-b-o/
bɔ ... tuutuu
hawk/-b-or ... -t-u-u-t-u-u/
bɔ birim
startle/-b-o-r -b-i-r-i-m/

bɔ dam
  go mad/-b-or -d-a-m/
bɔ mpae
  pray/-b-or -m-p-a-e/
bɔ nsamu
  clap/-b-or -n-s-a-m-u/
bɔ waw
  cough/-b-or -w-a-w/
bɔade
  creator/-b-or-a-d-e/
bɔaman
  conqueror/-b-or-a-m-a-n/
bɔbea
  shape/-b-or-b-e-a/
bɔbew
  disposition/-b-or-b-e-w/
bɔbo
  pick/-b-or-b-o/
bɔdambɔ
  bottle/-b-or-d-a-m-m-or/
bɔdes
  bodice/-b-or-d-e-s/
bɔdɔm
  dog/-k-r-a-m-a-n/
bɔdɛe
  fat/-b-or-d-er-e/
bɔfo
  courier/-b-or-f-o/
bɔgyɛte
  budget/-b-or-j-er-t-e/
Bɔkina Faso
  Burkina Faso/-b-or-k-i-n-a f-a-s-o/

Bɔkina Fasonyi
  Burkinabe/-b-or-k-i-n-a f-a-s-o-n-i-e/
bɔkɔɔ
  slowly/-b-or-k-or-or/
bɔmbɔnyi
  hunter/-b-or-m-m-or-n-i/
bɔn
  crow/-b-or-n/
bɔn
  pit/-b-or-n/
bɔn
  stink/-b-or-n/
bɔnamnyi
  butcher/-b-or-n-a-m-n-i/
bɔne
  sin/-b-or-n-e/
bɔne
  evil/-b-or-n-e/
bɔne
  bad/-b-or-n-e/
bɔnefakyɛ
  forgiveness/-b-or-n-e-f-a-ch-er/
bɔnka
  ditch/-b-or-n-k-a/
bɔnkɔ
  lobster/-b-or-n-k-or/
bɔnsa
  valley/-b-or-n-s-a/
bɔnwoma
  gall/-b-or-n-w-o-m-a/
bɔnyin
  barren/-b-or-n-i-n/

bɔɔfrɛ
  papaya/-b-o-r-o-r-f-r-e-r/
bɔɔl
  ball/-b-or-or-l/
bɔɔla
  dump/-b-or-or-l-a/
bɔɔlbɔ
  football/-b-or-or-l-b-or/
bɔre
  venom/-b-o-r-r-e/
bɔs
  bus/-b-or-s/
bɔsu
  dewdrop/-b-or-s-u/
bɔta
  butter/-b-or-t-a/
Bɔtswana
  Botswana/b-or-t-s-w-a-n-a/
Bɔtswananyi
  Motswana/b-or-t-s-w-a-n-a-n-i/
bɔtɔ
  pocket/-b-or-t-or/
bɔw
  fog/-b-or-w/
bɔw
  dew/-b-or-w/
bɔwen
  bile/-b-or-w-e-n/
bɔyeɛ
  hmph/-b-or-y-e-er/
bra
  come/-b-r-a/
bra

life/-b-r-a/
bra
  period/-b-r-a/
braban
  behaviour/-b-r-a-b-a-n/
brabere
  lifetime/-b-r-a-b-e-r-e/
bragoro
  sex education/-b-r-a-g-o-r-o/
brayaw
  dysmenorrhoea/-b-r-a-y-a-w/
Brazavel-Kongo
  Congo-Brazzaville/b-r-az-a-v-e-l-k-o-n-g-o/
Brazavel-Kongonyi
  Brazzaville-Congolese/b-r-az-a-v-e-l-k-o-n-g-o-n-i-e/
breeke
  brake/-b-r-e-e-k-e/
bregye
  bridge/-b-r-e-j-e/
brekese
  brick/-b-r-e-k-e-s-e/
brɛ
  tire/-b-r-e-r/
brɛ
  tiredness/-b-r-e-r/
brɛbo
  liver/-b-r-e-r-b-o/
brɛbo
  loyal/-b-r-e-r-b-o/
brɛbode
  loyalty/-b-r-e-r-b-o-d-e/

Bronya
  Christmas/-b-r-o-n-y-a/
brɔn
  area/-b-r-o-r-n/
Brunae
  Brunei/b-r-u-n-a-e/
Brunaenyi
  Bruneian/b-r-u-n-a-e-n-i/
bruu
  blue/-b-r-u-u/
bu
  respect/-b-u/
bu
  break/-b-u/
bu
  honour/-b-u/
bu ... man
  govern/-b-u ... -m-a-n/
bua
  respond/-b-u-a/
bubu
  smash/-b-u-b-u-o/
bubua
  lameness/-b-u-b-u-a/
bubuanyi
  cripple/-b-u-b-u-a-n-i/
buei
  open/-b-u-e-i/
bufalo
  buffalo/-b-u-f-a-l-o/
bukyia
  stove/-b-u-ch-i-a/
bukyia

  hearth/-b-u-ch-i-a/
bum
  plentiful/-b-u-m/
bun
  green/-b-u-n/
bura
  well/-b-u-r-a/
burabɔn
  borehole/-b-u-r-a-b-o-r-n/
buronyi
  foreigner/-b-u-r-o-n-i-e/
Burundi
  Burundi/b-u-r-u-n-n-i/
Burundinyi
  Burundian/b-u-r-u-n-n-i-n-i/
busu
  sacrilege/-b-u-s-u-o/
busua
  family/-b-u-s-u-a/
busuanyi
  relative/-b-u-s-u-a-n-i/
busuasanten
  genealogy/-b-u-s-u-a-s-a-n-t-e-n/
Butan
  Bhutan/b-u-t-a-n/
Butannyi
  Bhutann/b-u-t-a-n-n-i/
butuw
  overturn/-b-u-t-u-w/
buukuu
  book/-b-u-u-k-u-u/
buw
  coop/-b-u-w/

buwa
  roost/-b-u-w-a/
buwei
  excellent/-b-u-w-e-i/
d
  d/-d/
da
  sleep/-d-a/
da
  day/-d-a/
da
  never/-d-a/
da ... ase
  thank/-d-a ... -a-s-e/
da famu
  be trivial/-d-a -f-a-m-u/
da nkunkyire
  share bed with husband/-d-a
  -n-k-u-n-ch-i-r-e/
da yie
  sleep tight/-d-a -y-i-e/
daa
  daily/-d-a-a/
daadaa
  deceive/-d-a-a-d-a-a/
daadaa
  forever/-d-a-a-d-a-a/
daadaa
  disappoint/-d-a-a-d-a-a/
daade
  ground/-d-a-a-d-e/
daakye
  future/-d-a-a-ch-e/

daakyeadehu
  vision/-d-a-a-c-h-e-a-d-e-h-u/
dabodabo
  duck/-d-a-b-o-d-a-b-o/
dabraba
  falsification/-d-a-b-r-a-b-a/
dadaw
  old/-d-a-d-a-w/
dade
  iron/-d-a-d-e/
dade
  metal/-d-a-d-e/
dadewa
  nail/-d-a-d-e-w-a/
dado
  still/-d-a-d-o/
dae
  dream/-d-a-e/
daekɛse
  aspiration/-d-a-e-k-er-s-e/
daenoketew
  dinosaur/-d-a-e-n-o-k-e-t-e-w/
dame
  draughts/-d-a-m-e/
dampare
  roof/-d-a-m-p-a-r-e/
dan
  building/-d-a-n/
dan
  house/-d-a-n/
dan-kaw
  rent/-d-a-n-k-a-w/
dane

adapt/-d-a-n-e/
dane
transform/-d-a-n-e/
dapɛn
week/-d-a-p-er-n/
dasanyi
human/-d-a-s-a-n-i/
dase
testimony/-d-a-s-e/
dasenyi
witness/-d-a-s-e-n-i/
dawuro
gong gong/-d-a-w-u-r-o/
dawuru
news/-d-a-w-u-r-u-o/
dawurubɔ
proclamation/-d-a-w-u-r-u-b-o-r/
dawurubɔ-krataa
newspaper/-d-a-w-u-r-u-b-o-r-k-r-a-t-a-a/
de
have a hold on/-d-e/
de ... ba
bring/-d-e ... -b-a/
de ... kaw
owe/-d-e ... -k-a-w/
de ... mu
take hold of/-d-e ... -m-u/
de a ɛwɔ mu
content/-d-e -a -er-w-or -m-u/
dea
the thing/-a-d-e -n-o/

dea-ɛ-di-akyiri
next/-d-e-a-e-r-d-i-a-ch-i-r-i/
dea-ɛ-di-anyim
last/-d-e-a-er-d-i-a-n-i-m/
dea-ɛ-tɔso-abien
second/-d-e-a-er-t-or-s-o-a-b-i-e-n/
dea-ɛ-tɔso-du-akron
nineteenth/-d-e-a-e-r-t-o-r-s-o-d-u-a-k-r-o-n/
deda
lay/-d-e-d-a/
dede
noise/-d-e-d-e/
dede
sound/-d-e-d-e/
dededede
loud/-d-e-d-e-d-e-d-e/
dedepefee
clarion/-d-e-d-e-p-e-f-e-e/
dehye
user/-d-e-sh-e/
den
hard/-d-e-n/
dendene
solid/-d-e-n-n-e-n-e/
dendenndene
tightly/-d-e-n-n-e-n-n-n-e-n-e/
dene
difficult/-d-e-n-e/
dɛefo
philanthropist/-d-er-e-f-o/
dɛm

that/-d-er-m/
dɛm
scar/-d-er-m/
dɛm
whoa/-d-er-m/
dɛn
what/-d-er-n/
dɛnkyɛm
crocodile/-d-er-n-ch-er-m/
dɛnkyɛmbo
diamond/-d-er-n-ch-er-m-m-o/
dɛte
clay/-d-er-t-e/
dɛw
sweet/-d-er-w/
di
eat/-d-i/
di ... akohwi
lie/-d-i ... -a-k-o-h-w-i/
di ... akyiri
follow/-d-i ... -a-ch-i-r-i/
di ... ano
bargain/-d-i ... -a-n-o/
di ... fɔ
be guilty of/-d-i ... -f-or/
di ... hene
reign/-d-i ... -h-e-n-e/
di ... ho fɛw
tease/-d-i ... -h-o -f-er-w/
di ... kan
lead/-d-i ... -k-a-n/
di ... kyim
argue/-d-i ... -ch-i-m/

di ... kɔnkɔnsa
gossip/-d-i ... -k-or-n-k-or-n-s-a/
di ... nkonyim
triumph/-d-i ... -n-k-o-n-i-m/
di ... nyi
dignify/-d-i ... -n-i/
di ... nyim
win/-d-i ... -n-i-m/
di ... sa
battle/-d-i ... -s-a/
di ... so
control/-d-i ... -s-o/
di agoro
play/-d-i -a-g-o-r-o/
di ahurusi
exult/-d-i -a-h-u-r-u-s-i-e/
di bata
trade/-d-i -b-a-t-a/
di dɛw
rejoice/-d-i -d-er-w/
di mbuada
fast/-d-i -m-m-u-a-d-a/
di nkogu
be defeated/-d-i -n-k-o-g-u-o/
di nkɔmbɔ
converse/-d-i -n-k-or-m-m-or/
di yaw
grieve/-d-i -y-a-w/
di ɔdɔ
make love/-d-i -or-d-or/
dibew
position/-d-i-b-e-w/
didi

dine/-d-i-d-i/
Difuu
 August/d-i-f-u-u/
dimafo
 advocate/-d-i-m-a-f-o/
din
 noun/-d-i-n/
din
 name/-d-i-n/
dinhyɛananmu
 pronoun/-d-i-n-sh-er-a-n-a-n-m-u/
Dinka
 Dinka/d-i-n-k-a/
dinn
 quiet/-d-i-n-n/
dintamsi
 adjective/-d-i-n-t-a-m-s-i/
do
 on/-d-o/
dobɛ
 yaws/-d-o-b-er/
dodow
 quantity/-d-o-d-o-w/
dodow
 too much/-d-o-d-o-w/
dodow
 too/-d-o-d-o-w/
dondo
 squeeze drum/-d-o-n-n-o/
donkɔ
 slave/-d-o-n-k-or/
doroba

 needle/-d-o-r-o-b-a/
dɔ
 love/-d-or/
dɔ
 love/-d-or/
dɔfo
 darling/-d-or-f-o/
dɔfo
 beloved/-d-or-f-o/
dɔketa
 doctor/-d-or-k-e-t-a/
dɔkono
 kenkey/-d-or-k-o-n-o/
Dɔkye
 Dutch/d-or-ch-e/
dɔla
 dollar/-d-or-l-a/
dɔm
 crowd/-d-or-m/
dɔn
 hour/-d-or-n/
dɔnkyerɛ
 clock/-d-or-n-ch-e-r-e-r/
dɔɔso
 increase/-d-or-or-s-o/
dɔre
 thrive/-d-o-r-r-e/
dɔw
 weed/-d-or-w/
Dɔyekye
 German/d-or-y-e-ch-e/
drama
 drama/-d-r-a-m-a/

drɔw
  draw/-d-r-o-r-w/
drɔɔse
  drawers/-d-r-o-r-o-r-s-e/
du
  reach/-d-u/
du
  ten/-d-u/
du
  arrive/-d-u/
du-abiasa
  thirteen/-d-u-a-b-i-a-s-a/
du-abien
  twelve/-d-u-a-b-i-e-n/
du-akron
  nineteen/-d-u-a-k-r-o-n/
du-anan
  fourteen/-d-u-a-n-a-n/
du-anum
  fifteen/-d-u-a-n-u-m/
du-asia
  sixteen/-d-u-a-s-i-a/
du-asuon
  seventeen/-d-u-a-s-u-o-n/
du-awɔtwe
  eighteen/-d-u-a-w-or-t-w-e/
du-koro
  eleven/-d-u-k-o-r-o/
dua
  plant/-d-u-a/
dua
  enter/-d-u-a/
dua

  tail/-d-u-a/
dua
  tree/-d-u-a/
duaba
  stick/-d-u-a-b-a/
duabaa
  twig/-d-u-a-b-a-a/
duabo
  ebony/-d-u-a-b-o/
duado
  latrine/-d-u-a-d-o/
dudo
  boiled herbs/-d-u-d-o/
due
  condolences/-d-u-e/
dum
  turn off/-d-u-m/
dum
  extinguish/-d-u-m/
dumsɔ
  flicker/-d-u-m-s-or/
dunsinyi
  herbalist/-d-u-n-s-i-n-i/
duru
  weight/-d-u-r-u-o/
duruduru
  heavy/-d-u-r-u-d-u-r-u-o/
duukuu
  headscarf/-d-u-u-k-u-u/
dwe
  cool/-d-w-e/
dwe
  deflate/-d-w-e/

dwe
 nut/-d-w-e/
dwedwe
 calm/-d-w-e-d-w-e/
dwee
 cool/-d-w-e-e/
dwene
 think/-d-w-e-n-e/
dwetɛ
 silver/-d-w-e-t-er/
dwetɛ
 silver/-d-w-e-t-er/
dwɛɛ
 arrogant/-d-w-er-er/
dwɛɛtɛɛ
 cash/-d-w-er-er-t-er-er/
dwin
 construct/-d-w-i-n/
dwinnyi
 engineer/-d-w-i-n-n-i/
dwiriw
 crumble/-d-w-i-r-i-w/
dwonku
 hip/-d-w-o-n-k-u/
dwontonyi
 musician/-d-w-o-n-t-o-n-i-e/
dwow
 braid/-d-w-o-w/
Dwowda
 Monday/-d-w-o-w-d-a/
dwɔlɔf
 jollof/-d-w-or-l-or-f/
dwudwu

advantage/-d-w-u-d-w-u/
dwuma
 activity/-d-w-u-m-a/
dwumadi
 programme/-d-w-u-m-a-d-i/
dwumadi
 event/-d-w-u-m-a-d-i/
dwumayɛnyi
 worker/-d-w-u-m-a-y-er-n-i/
dwuw
 louse/-d-w-u-w/
dz
 z/-z/
dzɛn
 gentle/-z-er-n/
dzɛndzɛn
 gently/-z-er-n-nz-er-n/
e
 you/-e/
e
 ay/-e/
eban
 herring/-e-b-a-n/
eboa
 fishing-net/-e-b-o-a/
Ebɔbira
 April/e-b-o-r-b-i-r-a/
Ebɔw
 March/e-b-or-w/
efupɔnkɔ
 camel/-e-f-u-p-or-n-k-or/
enke
 ink/-e-n-k-e/

eno
 madam/-e-n-o/
eprikɔt
 apricot/-e-p-r-i-k-o-r-t/
eyam
 ringworm/-e-y-a-m/
ɛ
 it/-er/
ɛ
 e/-er/
ɛ te sɛn
 how do you are/-er -t-e -s-er-n/
ɛ te sɛn
 hello/-er -t-e -s-er-n/
ɛ-tɔ-da-bi-a
 sometimes/-er-t-or-d-a-b-i-a/
Ɛbɔ
 September/-ɛ-b-or/
ɛfirisɛ
 because/-e-r-f-i-r-i-s-e-r/
ɛgyerɛ
 gap/-e-r-j-e-r-e-r/
ɛkɔnɔmi
 economy/-er-k-or-n-or-m-i/
ɛkrɔ
 eczema/-e-r-k-r-o-r/
ɛno
 that thing/-a-d-e -d-er-m/
ɛno de
 in that case/-er-n-o -d-e/
Ɛritrea
 Eritrea/-ɛ-r-i-t-r-e-a/
Ɛritreani

Eritrean/-ɛ-r-i-t-r-e-a-n-i/
ɛspiriɛns
 experience/-e-r-s-p-i-r-i-e-r-n-s/
ɛwo
 honey/-er-w-o/
ɛwokyɛm
 honeycomb/-er-w-o-ch-er-m/
f
 f/-f/
fa
 part/-f-a/
fa
 half/-f-a/
fa
 take/-f-a/
fa
 page/-f-a/
fa
 keep/-f-a/
fa ... adamfo
 befriend/-f-a ... -a-d-a-m-f-o/
fa ... ho
 about/-f-a ... -h-o/
fa ... ho
 be relevant to/-f-a ... -h-o/
fa ... ka ho
 add/-f-a ... -k-a -h-o/
fa ... kyɛ
 forgive/-f-a ... -ch-er/
fa ... sesa
 exchange/-f-a ... -s-e-s-a/
fa ... to gua
 announce/-f-a ... -t-o -g-u-a/

faele
file/-f-a-e-l-e/
fafranta
butterfly/-f-a-f-r-a-n-t-a/
fam
attach/-f-a-m/
famu
floor/-f-a-m-u/
famufa
quarter/-f-a-m-u-f-a/
fan
cabbage/-f-a-n/
Fante
Fanti/-f-a-n-t-e/
fapem
foundation/-f-a-p-e-m/
farenyi
fisherman/-f-a-r-e-n-i/
fata
deserve/-f-a-t-a/
fawohodi
independence/-f-a-w-o-h-o-d-i-e/
fawohodi
freedom/-f-a-w-o-h-o-d-i-e/
fe
miss/-f-e/
fe
vomit/-f-e/
fe
vomit/-f-e/
feaa
thin/-f-e-a-a/

fefa
caress/-f-e-f-a/
fefuw
sprout/-f-e-f-u-w/
fefɛwbere
spring/-f-e-f-e-r-w-b-e-r-e/
fekyere
adjust/-f-e-ch-e-r-e/
fekyew
doctor/-f-e-ch-e-w/
Felepins
Philippines/f-e-l-e-p-i-n-s/
Felepinsnyi
Filipino/f-e-l-e-p-i-n-s-n-i/
fere
melon/-f-e-r-e/
feseks
physics/-f-e-s-e-k-s/
few
kiss/-f-e-w/
fɛ
peer/-f-er/
fɛkuw
association/-f-er-k-u-w/
fɛm
lend/-f-er-m/
fɛnsere
window/-f-e-r-n-s-e-r-e/
fɛre
shyness/-f-e-r-r-e/
fɛre
be shy/-f-e-r-r-e/
fɛw

beautiful/-f-er-w/
fɛwfɛw
pretty/-f-er-w-f-er-w/
fi
from/-f-i/
fi
depart/-f-i/
fiade
prison/-f-i-a-d-e/
fiase
jail/-f-i-a-s-e/
Fida
Friday/-f-i-d-a/
fie
home/-f-i-e/
fiewura
landlord/-f-i-e-w-u-r-a/
fifiri
germinate/-f-i-f-i-r-i/
fih
dirt/-f-i-h/
fih
dirty/-f-i-h/
fiise
fees/-f-i-i-s-e/
fikyiri
backyard/-f-i-ch-i-r-i/
finimfin
centre/-f-i-n-i-m-f-i-n/
fintiw
stumble/-f-i-n-t-i-w/
firi
borrow/-f-i-r-i/

firikyiwa
castanet/-f-i-r-i-ch-i-w-a/
fitaa
white/-f-i-t-a-a/
fiti
since/-f-i-t-i/
fitia
bungalow/-f-i-t-i-a/
flɔriin
fluorine/-f-l-o-r-r-i-i-n/
fo
cheap/-f-o/
foforo
new/-f-o-f-o-r-o/
fom
err/-f-o-m/
fon
stupid/-f-o-n/
foonoo
oven/-f-o-o-n-o-o/
fora
mix/-f-o-r-a/
foto
photograph/-f-o-t-o/
fow
climb/-f-o-w/
fɔkyee
soaked/-f-or-ch-e-e/
fɔɔke
fork/-f-or-or-k-e/
fɔsefɔrɔs
phosphorus/-f-o-r-s-e-f-o-r-r-o-r-s/

fɔw
  get wet/-f-or-w/
fɔwee
  wet/-f-or-w-e-e/
frankaa
  flag/-f-r-a-n-k-a-a/
Frans
  France/f-r-a-n-s/
fregye
  fridge/-f-r-e-j-e/
frɛ
  call/-f-r-e-r/
frɛnkye
  French/-f-r-e-r-n-ch-e/
Frɛnkyenyi
  French/f-r-e-r-n-ch-e-n-i/
frɔwee
  stew/-f-r-o-r-w-e-e/
fua
  support/-f-u-a/
fufu
  fufu/-f-u-f-u-o/
Fula
  Fula/f-u-l-a/
funu
  corpse/-f-u-n-u-o/
funu
  useless/-f-u-n-u-o/
fura
  cover/-f-u-r-a/
fuw
  overgrow/-f-u-w/
g

g/-g/
gaaleke
  garlic/-g-a-a-l-e-k-e/
Gaana
  Ghana/g-a-a-n-a/
Gaananyi
  Ghanaian/g-a-a-n-a-n-i/
gaas
  gas/-g-a-a-s/
gaas
  gaseous/-g-a-a-s/
Gabɔn
  Gabon/g-a-b-or-n/
Gabɔnnyi
  Gabonese/g-a-b-or-n-n-i/
galɔn
  gallon/-g-a-l-or-n/
Gambia
  Gambia/g-a-m-m-i-a/
Gambianyi
  Gambian/g-a-m-m-i-a-n-i/
garagye
  garage/-g-a-r-a-j-e/
gari
  gari/-g-a-r-i/
Gaza
  Gaza/g-az-a/
Gazanyi
  Gazan/g-az-a-n-i/
Gbe
  Gbe/g-b-e/
geeti
  gate/-g-e-e-t-i/

Gini
Guinea/g-i-n-i/
Gininyi
Guinean/g-i-n-i-n-i/
gol
goal/-g-o-l/
gon
gray/-g-o-n/
gow
soften/-g-o-w/
gowgow
soft/-g-o-w-g-o-w/
gɔta
gutter/-g-or-t-a/
gram
gramme/-g-r-a-m/
gu
annul/-g-u/
gu ... anyim ase
disgrace/-g-u ... -a-n-i-m -a-s-e/
gu ... ho fi
defile/-f-i -g-u ... -h-o/
gu ahome
breathe/-g-u -a-h-o-m-e/
gu nsu
urinate/-g-u -n-s-u/
gua
market/-g-u-a/
gua
shopping/-g-u-a/
guade
product/-g-u-a-d-e/
guadi

business/-g-u-a-d-i/
guamba
lamb/-g-u-a-m-m-a/
guamudawurbɔ
ad/-g-u-a-m-u-d-a-w-u-r-b-o-r/
guamutenanyi
chairperson/-g-u-a-m-u-t-e-n-a-n-i/
guan
sheep/-g-u-a-n/
guane
flee/-g-u-a-n-e/
guankɔbea
refuge/-g-u-a-n-k-or-b-e-a/
guare
bathe/-g-u-a-r-e/
guatiri
investment/-g-u-a-t-i-r-i/
gunsu
urine/-g-u-n-s-u/
gurannsera
lemon/-g-u-r-a-n-n-s-e-r-a/
gy
j/-j/
gya
leave/-j-a/
gya
fire/-j-a/
gya ... kwan
see ... off/-j-a ... -q-a-n/
gya ... kwan
guide/-j-a ... -q-a-n/
gyaade

kitchen/-j-a-a-d-e/
gyae
cease/-j-a-e/
gyae ... to famu
drop/-j-a-e ... -t-o -f-a-m-u/
gyagowa
jaguar/-j-a-g-o-w-a/
gyama
maybe/-j-a-m-a/
gyama
jama/-j-a-m-a/
Gyameika
Jamaica/g-y-a-m-e-i-k-a/
gyan
wasted/-j-a-n/
gyanka
orphan/-j-a-n-k-a/
Gyapan
Japan/g-y-a-p-a-n/
Gyapannyi
Japanese/g-y-a-p-a-n-n-i/
gyasaaboafo
tiger/-j-a-s-a-a-b-o-a-f-o/
gyaye
free/-j-a-y-e/
gye
collect/-j-e/
gye
except/-j-e/
gye
get/-j-e/
gye
rescue/-j-e/

gye ... ahome
rest/-j-e ... -a-h-o-m-e/
gye ... akyingye
dispute/-j-e ... -a-ch-i-n-j-e/
gye ... anyi
entertain/-j-e ... -a-n-i/
gye ... di
believe/-j-e ... -d-i/
gye ... to mu
accept/-j-e ... -t-o -m-u/
gye ... yɛn
adopt/-j-e ... -y-er-n/
gye din
become famous/-j-e -d-i-n/
gyedi
faith/-j-e-d-i/
gyegye
annoy/-j-e-j-e/
gyengyɛn
unnecessary/-j-e-n-j-er-n/
gyensɛn
ginseng/-j-e-n-s-er-n/
gyerasee
glass/-j-e-r-a-s-e-e/
Gyeɔgyea
Georgia/-j-e-or-j-e-a/
Gyeɔgyeanyi
Georgian/-j-e-or-j-e-a-n-i/
Gyɛmɛni
Germany/g-y-er-m-er-n-i/
Gyibuti
Djibouti/g-y-i-b-u-t-i-e/
Gyibutinyi

Djiboutian/g-y-i-b-u-t-i-n-i/
gyimi
jest/-j-i-m-i/
gyimi
jester/-j-i-m-i/
gyiminyi
idiot/-j-i-m-i-n-i/
gyina
stand/-j-i-n-a/
gyinabea
stop/-j-i-n-a-b-e-a/
gyinabew
state/-j-i-n-a-b-e-w/
gyinae
decision/-j-i-n-a-e/
gyinse
jeans/-j-i-n-s-e/
gyirafe
giraffe/-j-i-r-a-f-e/
h
h/-h/
ha
here/-h-a/
ha
here/-h-a/
haban
plant/-h-a-b-a-n/
haedrogyen
hydrogen/-h-a-e-d-r-o-j-e-n/
haedrogyen
hydrogen/-h-a-e-d-r-o-j-e-n/
Haelaefe
highlife/h-a-e-l-a-e-f-e/

hahyetage
hashtag/-h-a-sh-e-t-a-g-e/
hamɛr
hammer/-h-a-m-e-r-r/
hankete
handkerchief/-h-a-n-k-e-t-e/
hann
light/-h-a-n-n/
hare
speed/-h-a-r-e/
hare
lightweight/-h-a-r-e/
hata
dry/-h-a-t-a/
hataw
leaf/-h-a-t-a-w/
haw
bother/-h-a-w/
haw
bother/-h-a-w/
haw
worry/-h-a-w/
Hawosa
Hausa/h-a-w-o-s-a/
hembaa
queen/-h-e-m-m-a-a/
hemfa
where/-h-e-m-f-a/
hen
king/-h-e-n/
hene
chief/-h-e-n-e/
Heplaefe

hiplife/h-e-p-l-a-e-f-e/
hɛmba
  canoe/-h-er-m-m-a/
hɛn
  our/-h-er-n/
hɛn
  us/-h-er-n/
hɛnde
  ours/-h-er-n-n-e/
hɛnho
  ourselves/-h-er-n-h-o/
hɛnkani
  driver/-h-er-n-k-a-n-i/
hia
  need/-h-i-a/
hia
  poverty/-h-i-a/
hiade
  need/-h-i-a-d-e/
hiani
  indigent/-h-i-a-n-i/
hihim
  vibrate/-h-i-h-i-m/
hiliyɔm
  helium/-h-i-l-i-y-or-m/
him
  sway/-h-i-m/
hinhim
  rock/-h-i-n-h-i-m/
ho
  by/-h-o/
ho
  around/-h-o/

ho
  self/-h-o/
hoa
  fade/-h-o-a/
hohoro
  launder/-h-o-h-o-r-o/
hokafo
  spouse/-h-o-k-a-f-o/
hoku
  suicide/-h-o-k-u-o/
hokwan
  access/-h-o-q-a-n/
hom
  your/-h-o-m/
hom
  you/-h-o-m/
hom
  you/-h-o-m/
homde
  yours/-h-o-m-d-e/
homeda
  holiday/-h-o-m-e-d-a/
honam
  flesh/-h-o-n-a-m/
honamanyi
  skin/-h-o-n-a-m-a-n-i/
honamdua
  body/-h-o-n-a-m-d-u-a/
honhom
  spirit/-h-o-n-h-o-m/
hono
  swell/-h-o-n-o/
hɔ

there/-h-or/

hɔ
there/-h-or/

hɔho
guest/-h-or-h-o/

hɔn
their/-h-or-n/

hɔn
them/-h-or-n/

hɔnho
themselves/-h-or-n-h-o/

hram
yawn/-h-r-a-m/

hu
see/-h-u/

hu
scary/-h-u/

hu
find/-h-u/

hu ... ansa
foresee/-h-u ... -a-n-s-a/

hu ... mbobɔr
show ... pity/-h-u ... -m-m-o-b-o-r-r/

hu amande
suffer/-h-u -a-m-a-n-n-e/

hua
smell/-h-u-a/

huahuam
fragrant/-h-u-a-h-u-a-m/

huam
fragrance/-h-u-a-m/

huam nkrɔm

snore/-h-u-a-m -n-k-r-o-r-m/

huane
peel/-h-u-a-n-e/

huei
pour/-h-u-e-i/

huhuuhu
frightening/-h-u-h-u-u-h-u-o/

huna
frighten/-h-u-n-a/

hunti
sneeze/-h-u-n-t-i/

huntuma
soot/-h-u-n-t-u-m-a/

hunu
empty/-h-u-n-u-o/

huoo
blazing/-h-u-o-o/

hurae
malaria/-h-u-r-a-e/

hurow
shame/-h-u-r-o-w/

huru
boil/-h-u-r-u-o/

hurututu
lung/-h-u-r-u-t-u-t-u-o/

huruw
jump/-h-u-r-u-w/

husu
reflection/-h-u-s-u-o/

huw
blow/-h-u-w/

hwe
spank/-h-w-e/

hwe ase
 fall down/-h-w-e -a-s-e/
hweaa
 slim/-h-w-e-a-a/
hwee
 nothing/-h-w-e-e/
hweeara
 zero/-h-w-e-e-a-r-a/
hwehwɛ
 search/-h-w-e-h-w-er/
hwehwɛ
 seek/-h-w-e-h-w-er/
hwene
 nose/-h-w-e-n-e/
hwentea
 xylopia/-h-w-e-n-t-e-a/
hwenteaba
 clove/-h-w-e-n-t-e-a-b-a/
hwere
 lose/-h-w-e-r-e/
hwere
 duration/-h-w-e-r-e/
hwɛ
 watch/-h-w-er/
hwɛ
 look/-h-w-er/
hwɛ ... so
 manage/-h-w-er ... -s-o/
hwɛ ... so yie
 maintain/-h-w-er ... -s-o -y-i-e/
hwɛ ... yie
 take care/-h-w-er ... -y-i-e/
hwɛ ... yie

 care/-h-w-er ... -y-i-e/
hwɛyiehwɛyie
 careful/-h-w-er-y-i-e-h-w-er-y-i-e/
hwi
 hair/-h-w-i/
hwiir
 wheel/-h-w-i-i-r/
hwim
 snatch/-h-w-i-m/
hwirow
 slurp/-h-w-i-r-o-w/
hwiruow
 suck/-h-w-i-r-u-o-w/
hy
 sh/-sh/
hye gyama
 sing jama/-sh-e -j-a-m-a/
hyee
 fast/-sh-e-e/
hyehye
 burn/-sh-e-sh-e/
hyehyew
 scald/-sh-e-sh-e-w/
hyehyɛ
 arrange/-sh-e-sh-er/
hyehyɛ ... ahoroba
 diss/-sh-e-sh-e-r ... -a-h-o-r-o-b-a/
hyehyɛpɛ
 civilized/-sh-e-sh-er-p-er/
hyera
 vase/-sh-e-r-a/
hyeren
 shine/-sh-e-r-e-n/

hyew
hot/-sh-e-w/
hyew
incinerate/-sh-e-w/
hyew
heat/-sh-e-w/
hyewhyew
active/-sh-e-w-sh-e-w/
Hyeɔna
Shona/h-y-e-or-n-a/
hyɛ
nominate/-sh-er/
hyɛ
wear/-sh-er/
hyɛ
force/-sh-er/
hyɛ
command/-sh-er/
hyɛ
score/-sh-er/
hyɛ ... ahoroba
insult/-sh-e-r ... -a-h-o-r-o-b-a/
hyɛ ... ananmu
replace/-sh-er ... -a-n-a-n-m-u/
hyɛ ... anyimunyam
honour/-sh-er ... -a-n-i-m-u-n-y-a-m/
hyɛ ... ase
start/-sh-er ... -a-s-e/
hyɛ ... ase
begin/-sh-er ... -a-s-e/
hyɛ ... den
strengthen/-sh-er ... -d-e-n/

hyɛ ... do
oppress/-sh-er ... -d-o/
hyɛ ... ma
fill up/-sh-er ... -m-a/
hyɛ ... ma
fill/-sh-er ... -m-a/
hyɛ ... nkuran
encourage/-sh-e-r ... -n-k-u-r-a-n/
hyɛ ase yɛ
become/-sh-er -a-s-e -y-er/
hyɛ da
pretend/-sh-er -d-a/
hyɛ nkɔm
prophesy/-sh-er -n-k-or-m/
hyɛe
line/-sh-er-e/
hyɛfe
chef/-sh-er-f-e/
hyɛn
vehicle/-sh-er-n/
hyɛn-gyinabea
port/-sh-er-n-j-i-n-a-b-e-a/
hyɛnhyɛmbo
criestal/-sh-er-n-sh-er-m-m-o/
hyɛpɛɛ
ostentatious/-sh-er-p-er-er/
hyɛɛte
shirt/-sh-er-er-t-e/
hyia
meet/-sh-i-a/
hyiahiano
congenial/-sh-i-a-h-i-a-n-o/

hyira
bless/-sh-i-r-a/
i
ee/-i/
Ibo
Igbo/i-b-o/
ibola
ebola/-i-b-o-l-a/
Id
Eid/i-d/
ilɛktrɔn
electron/-i-l-e-r-k-t-r-o-r-n/
imel
email/-i-m-e-l/
India
India/-i-n-n-i-a/
India
Indian/-i-n-n-i-a/
Indianyi
Indian/-i-n-n-i-a-n-i/
indigo
indigo/-i-n-n-i-g-o/
Indonihyia
Indonesia/-i-n-n-o-n-i-sh-i-a/
Indonihyianyi
Indonesian/-i-n-n-o-n-i-sh-i-a-n-i/
ingyin
engine/-i-n-j-i-n/
intanɛte
internet/-i-n-t-a-n-er-t-e/
Irak
Iraq/i-r-a-k/

Iraknyi
Iraqi/-i-r-a-k-n-i/
Iran
Iran/i-r-a-n/
Irannyi
Iranian/-i-r-a-n-n-i/
Israɛl
Israel/i-s-r-a-e-r-l/
Israɛlnyi
Israeli/-i-s-r-a-e-r-l-n-i/
Italiya
Italy/-i-t-a-l-i-y-a/
Jɔɔdan
Jordan/j-or-or-d-a-n/
Jɔɔdannyi
Jordanian/j-or-or-d-a-n-n-i/
k
k/-k/
ka
tell/-k-a/
ka
bite/-k-a/
ka
speak/-k-a/
ka
touch/-k-a/
ka
drive/-k-a/
ka ... bom
unite/-k-a ... -b-o-m/
ka ... fra   mu
integrate/-k-a ... -f-r-a -m-u/
ka ... ho

hurry/-k-a ... -h-o/
ka ... hyew
stimulate/-k-a ... -sh-e-w/
ka ... ntam
swear/-k-a ... -n-t-a-m/
ka wo ano
taste/-k-a -w-o -a-n-o/
kaabɔn
carbon/-k-a-a-b-or-n/
kaade
card/-k-a-a-d-e/
kaansa
though/-k-a-a-n-s-a/
kaar
car/-k-a-a-r/
kaasɛ
figure/-k-a-a-s-er/
kaaton
carton/-k-a-a-t-o-n/
kaatun
cartoon/-k-a-a-t-u-n/
kabea
tense/-k-a-b-e-a/
kabum
explode/-k-a-b-u-m/
kae
remember/-k-a-e/
kafamu
land/-k-a-f-a-m-u/
kafra
excuse me/-k-a-f-r-a/
kakaduru
ginger/-k-a-k-a-d-u-r-u-o/

kakae
apparition/-k-a-k-a-e/
kakae
monster/-k-a-k-a-e/
kakarika
cockroach/-k-a-k-a-r-i-k-a/
kakaw
toothache/-k-a-k-a-w/
kakii
khakhi/-k-a-k-i-i/
kakra
little/-k-a-k-r-a/
kakra
a little/-k-a-k-r-a/
kakraabi
a bit/-k-a-k-r-a-a-b-i/
kakraba
smallest/-k-a-k-r-a-b-a/
kakraka
large/-k-a-k-r-a-k-a/
kala
colour/-k-a-l-a/
kalsiyɔm
calcium/-k-a-l-s-i-y-or-m/
kalɛnda
calendar/-k-a-l-er-n-n-a/
kama
delightful/-k-a-m-a/
kamakamakama
best/-k-a-m-a-k-a-m-a-k-a-m-a/
kamayɛ
quality/-k-a-m-a-y-er/
Kambodia

Cambodia/-k-a-m-m-o-d-i-a/
Kambodianyi
Cambodian/-k-a-m-m-o-d-i-a-n-i/
kame
deny/-k-a-m-e/
kamera
camera/-k-a-m-e-r-a/
Kamerun
Cameroon/-k-a-m-e-r-u-n/
kamfo
commend/-k-a-m-f-o/
kamin
cumin/-k-a-m-i-n/
kamomael
chamomile/-k-a-m-o-m-a-e-l/
kampen
campaign/-k-a-m-p-e-n/
kan
count/-k-a-n/
kan
read/-k-a-n/
Kanada
Canada/-k-a-n-a-d-a/
kandea
lantern/-k-a-n-n-e-a/
kandinyi
trailblazer/-k-a-n-n-i-n-i/
kane
first/-k-a-n-e/
kanee
number/-k-a-n-e-e/
kankabi
poisonous/-k-a-n-k-a-b-i/

kankan
pungently/-k-a-n-k-a-n/
kanko
circle/-k-a-n-k-o/
kann
bright/-k-a-n-n/
kapentadwuma
carpentry/-k-a-p-e-n-t-a-d-w-u-m-a/
kapentanyi
carpenter/-k-a-p-e-n-t-a-n-i/
kapɛt
carpet/-k-a-p-er-t/
kari
weigh/-k-a-r-i/
Karibiyɛn
Caribbean/-k-a-r-i-b-i-y-e-r-n/
karɔte
carrot/-k-a-r-o-r-t-e/
kasa
language/-k-a-s-a/
kasa
talk/-k-a-s-a/
kasabisa
debate/-k-a-s-a-b-i-s-a/
kasafiri
radio/-k-a-s-a-f-i-r-i/
kasafua
word/-k-a-s-a-f-u-a/
kasahare
rap/-k-a-s-a-h-a-r-e/
kasakyerɛmunyi
interpreter/-k-a-s-a-ch-e-r-e-r-m-

u-n-i-e/
kasamafo
lawyer/-*k-a-s-a-m-a-f-o*/
kasambirenyi
figure of speech/-*k-a-s-a-m-m-i-r-e-n-i*/
kasaprɛko
authoritative/-*k-a-s-a-p-r-e-r-k-o*/
kasasua
dictionary/-*k-a-s-a-s-u-a*/
Kataa
Qatar/*k-a-t-a-a*/
Kataanyi
Qatari/*k-a-t-a-a-n-i*/
katakyi
valiant/-*k-a-t-a-ch-i*/
katakyi
warrior/-*k-a-t-a-ch-i*/
katakyi
brave/-*k-a-t-a-ch-i*/
katakyi
champion/-*k-a-t-a-ch-i*/
kaw
negative/-*k-a-w*/
kaw
cost/-*k-a-w*/
kaw
debt/-*k-a-w*/
kawa
ring/-*k-a-w-a*/
kawokye
couch/-*k-a-w-o-ch-e*/

kaya
porter/-*k-a-y-a*/
Kazakestan
Kazakhstan/-*k-az-a-k-e-s-t-a-n*/
Kazakestannyi
Kazakhstani/-*k-az-a-k-e-s-t-a-n-n-i*/
kebii
pitch black/-*k-e-b-i-i*/
keka
cause itchiness/-*k-e-k-a*/
keka
insinuate/-*k-e-k-a*/
keka mu
shout/-*k-e-k-a -m-u*/
kente
kente/-*k-e-n-t-e*/
Kenya
Kenya/*k-e-n-y-a*/
kenyan
revive/-*k-e-n-y-a-n*/
Keregezestan
Kyrgyzstan/*k-e-r-e-g-ez-e-s-t-a-n*/
Keregezestannyi
Kyrgyzstani/*k-e-r-e-g-ez-e-s-t-a-n-n-i*/
kete
small/-*k-e-t-e*/
ketee
strongly/-*k-e-t-e-e*/
keteke
train/-*k-e-t-e-k-e*/

ketekekwan
railway/-k-e-t-e-k-e-q-a-n/
ketekete
tiny/-k-e-t-e-k-e-t-e/
keteketepaa
minimum/-k-e-t-e-k-e-t-e-p-a-a/
ketew
lizard/-k-e-t-e-w/
ketewa
little/-k-e-t-e-w-a/
kɛɛten
curtain/-k-er-er-t-e-n/
kɛkɛ
just/-k-er-k-er/
kɛmistiri
chemistry/-k-e-r-m-i-s-t-i-r-i/
kɛntɛn
basket/-k-er-n-t-er-n/
kɛntɛn-bɔɔlbɔ
basketball/-k-er-n-t-er-n-b-or-or-l-b-or/
kɛse
big/-k-er-s-e/
kɛse
great/-k-er-s-e/
kɛsepaa
maximum/-k-er-s-e-p-a-a/
kɛtɛ
mat/-k-er-t-er/
kɛtɛasehyɛ
bribery/-k-er-t-er-a-s-e-sh-er/
kiibɔd
keyboard/-k-i-i-b-or-d/

kilomita
kilometer/-k-i-l-o-m-i-t-a/
Kinhyɛasa-Kongo
Congo-Kinshasa/k-i-n-sh-er-a-s-a-k-o-n-g-o/
kita
hold/-k-i-t-a/
kita ... ho
clean/-k-i-t-a ... -h-o/
kleke
click/-k-l-e-k-e/
klorin
chlorine/-k-l-o-r-i-n/
ko
fight/-k-o/
koa
bend/-k-o-a/
kodi
fable/-k-o-d-i-e/
Kofi
Kofi/k-o-f-i-e/
kohwi
deception/-k-o-h-w-i/
kohwinyi
liar/-k-o-h-w-i-n-i/
koko
easy/-k-o-k-o/
koko
hill/-k-o-k-o/
kokoa
private/-k-o-k-o-a/
kokoa
corner/-k-o-k-o-a/

kokoamusɛm
  privacy/-k-o-k-o-a-m-u-s-er-m/
kokonte
  kokonte/-k-o-k-o-n-t-e/
kokoo
  cocoa/-k-o-k-o-o/
kokoram
  cancer/-k-o-k-o-r-a-m/
kokromoti
  thumb/-k-o-k-r-o-m-o-t-i-e/
kokwa
  smoothen/-k-o-q-a/
kolegyi
  college/-k-o-l-e-j-i/
koliko
  puppet/-k-o-l-i-k-o/
komm
  silent/-k-o-m-m/
kommyɛ
  silence/-k-o-m-m-y-er/
Kongo
  Kongo/k-o-n-g-o/
Kongo
  Congo/k-o-n-g-o/
konko
  tin/-k-o-n-k-o/
kontaa
  account/-k-o-n-t-a-a/
kontombire
  cocoyam leaves/-k-o-n-t-o-m-m-i-r-e/
kontompo
  perjury/-k-o-n-t-o-m-p-o/

kontoromfi
  chimpanzee/-k-o-n-t-o-r-o-m-f-i/
koobi
  salted fish/-k-o-o-b-i-e/
koodu
  code/-k-o-o-d-u-o/
kooko
  porridge/-k-o-o-k-o/
kookyi
  coach/-k-o-o-ch-i/
kootaa
  coaltar/-k-o-o-t-a-a/
kootu
  coat/-k-o-o-t-u-o/
kora
  preserve/-k-o-r-a/
kora
  rival/-k-o-r-a/
koraa
  totally/-k-o-r-a-a/
korabo
  bullet/-k-o-r-a-b-o/
koran
  koran/-k-o-r-a-n/
koratwe
  rivalry/-k-o-r-a-t-w-e/
korbata
  branch/-k-o-r-b-a-t-a/
kore
  herpes/-k-o-r-e/
koro
  one/-k-o-r-o/
koroso

another/-k-o-r-o-s-o/
korotee
sole/-k-o-r-o-t-e-e/
koroyɛ
unity/-k-o-r-o-y-e-r/
korɔn
height/-k-o-r-o-r-n/
kosua
egg/-k-o-s-u-a/
kosɛ
sorry/-k-o-s-er/
kotiko
hiccups/-k-o-t-i-k-o/
kotodwe
knee/-k-o-t-o-d-w-e/
kotokrodo
wasp/-k-o-t-o-k-r-o-d-o/
kotoku
sack/-k-o-t-o-k-u-o/
kotow
squat/-k-o-t-o-w/
kɔ
go/-k-or/
kɔ ... mu
log in/-k-or ... -m-u/
kɔ tiefi
go to the toilet/-k-or -t-i-e-f-i/
kɔannkɔ
recurring/-k-or-a-n-n-k-or/
kɔbea
trend/-k-or-b-e-a/
kɔdu
to/-k-or-d-u/

kɔen
coin/-k-or-e-n/
kɔfe
coffee/-k-or-f-e/
kɔkɔ
warning/-k-or-k-or/
kɔkɔɔ
red/-k-or-k-or-or/
kɔm
hunger/-k-or-m/
kɔma
comma/-k-or-m-a/
kɔmfo
prophet/-k-or-m-f-o/
kɔmpiyuta
computer/-k-or-m-p-i-y-u-t-a/
Kɔmɔrɔs
Komoros/-k-o-r-m-o-r-r-o-r-s/
Kɔmɔrɔsnyi
Comoran/k-o-r-m-o-r-r-o-r-s-n-i/
kɔn
neck/-k-or-n/
kɔndɔ
desire/-k-or-n-n-or/
kɔnmuade
necklace/-k-or-n-m-u-a-d-e/
kɔnomnsanyi
drunkard/-k-or-n-o-m-n-s-a-n-i/
kɔnomtii
committee/-k-or-n-o-m-t-i-i/
kɔɔpow
cup/-k-or-or-p-o-w/
kɔr

proceed/-k-o-r-r/
kɔsidɛ
until/-k-or-s-i-d-er/
kɔsɔɔ
gaudy/-k-or-s-or-or/
kɔte
penis/-k-or-t-e/
kɔtɔ
crab/-k-or-t-or/
kɔtɔkɔ
porcupine/-k-or-t-or-k-or/
kra
say goodbye/-k-r-a/
kra
soul/-k-r-a/
kraban
giant/-k-r-a-b-a-n/
krado
ready/-k-r-a-d-o/
krakun
turkey/-k-r-a-k-u-n/
krakye
gentleman/-k-r-a-ch-e/
kramo
Islamic/-k-r-a-m-o/
kramonyi
muslim/-k-r-a-m-o-n-i-e/
kramosom
Islam/-k-r-a-m-o-s-o-m/
krataa
paper/-k-r-a-t-a-a/
kratebiew
spine/-k-r-a-t-e-b-i-e-w/

kratebiew-ahuon-ntini
spinal cord/-k-r-a-t-e-b-i-e-w-a-h-u-o-n-n-t-i-n-i/
kresiin
kerosene/-k-r-e-s-i-i-n/
Kristo
Christ/k-r-i-s-t-o/
kristonyi
Christian/-k-r-i-s-t-o-n-i-e/
kristosom
Christianity/-k-r-i-s-t-o-s-o-m/
krowa
calabash/-k-r-o-w-a/
krɔkrɔw
lock/-k-r-o-r-k-r-o-r-w/
krɔn
solemn/-k-r-o-r-n/
krɔn
be high/-k-r-o-r-n/
krɔnkrɔn
holy/-k-r-o-r-n-k-r-o-r-n/
krɔnoo
burglary/-k-r-o-r-n-o-o/
ks
x/-k-s/
ku
kill/-k-u/
kua
kindle/-k-u-a/
kua
farm/-k-u-a/
kuanyi
farmer/-k-u-a-n-i/

kube
  coconut/-k-u-b-e/
kukuduuduw
  bud/-k-u-k-u-d-u-u-d-u-w/
kukuru
  wield/-k-u-k-u-r-u-o/
kukuw
  stump/-k-u-k-u-w/
kuma
  smaller/-k-u-m-a/
kuna
  widowed/-k-u-n-a/
kuna
  widowhood/-k-u-n-a/
kunafo
  widower/-k-u-n-a-f-o/
kuntann
  huge/-k-u-n-t-a-n-n/
kuntu
  blanket/-k-u-n-t-u/
kunu
  husband/-k-u-n-u-o/
kupa
  copper/-k-u-p-a/
kur
  roof/-k-u-r/
kura
  mouse/-k-u-r-a/
kuraba
  potty/-k-u-r-a-b-a/
kurow
  town/-k-u-r-o-w/
kurowkɛse

  city/-k-u-r-o-w-k-e-r-s-e/
kurowmu
  hometown/-k-u-r-o-w-m-u/
kuru
  sore/-k-u-r-u-o/
kurukuruwafa
  hemisphere/-k-u-r-u-k-u-r-u-w-a-f-a/
kusi
  rat/-k-u-s-i-e/
kutonyi
  helmsman/-k-u-t-o-n-i-e/
kutow
  steer/-k-u-t-o-w/
kutu
  pot/-k-u-t-u-o/
kutuku
  blow/-k-u-t-u-k-u-o/
kutuku
  fist/-k-u-t-u-k-u-o/
kutukubɔ
  boxing/-k-u-t-u-k-u-b-or/
kuubu
  cube/-k-u-u-b-u-o/
kuw
  gang/-k-u-w/
kuwbu
  administration/-k-u-w-b-u/
Kuweti
  Kuwait/k-u-w-e-t-i/
Kuwetinyi
  Kuwaiti/k-u-w-e-t-i-n-i/
kuwu

heap/-k-u-w-u-o/
kw
q/-q/
kwa
waste/-q-a/
kwa
mere/-q-a/
kwa
free/-q-a/
kwaadonto
sluggard/-q-a-a-d-o-n-t-o/
kwaadu
indictment/-q-a-a-d-u/
kwaakwaa
raucously/-q-a-a-q-a-a/
Kwabena
Kobina/k-w-a-b-e-n-a/
kwabran
capable/-q-a-b-r-a-n/
kwadu
banana/-q-a-d-u/
kwadum
powder-keg/-q-a-d-u-m/
Kwadwo
Kojo/k-w-a-d-w-o/
kwadwom
lamentation/-q-a-d-w-o-m/
kwae
forest/-q-a-e/
kwaedu
ox/-q-a-e-d-u/
Kwaku
Kweku/-k-w-a-k-u/

Kwakwar
February/-q-a-q-a-r/
Kwame
Kwame/k-w-a-m-e/
kwan
road/-q-a-n/
kwan
way/-q-a-n/
kwan
row/-q-a-n/
kwangyanyi
guide/-q-a-n-j-a-n-i/
kwankyerɛnyi
leader/-q-a-n-ch-e-r-e-r-n-i/
kwansera
espionage/-q-a-n-s-e-r-a/
kwanseranyi
spy/-q-a-n-s-e-r-a-n-i/
kwansin
mile/-q-a-n-s-i-n/
kwansiw
obstacle/-q-a-n-s-i-w/
kwanso brɛbrɛ
safe travels/-q-a-n-s-o-b-r-e-r-b-r-e-r/
kwanta
ladle/-q-a-n-t-a/
kwantemfi
highway/-q-a-n-t-e-m-f-i/
kwantunyi
traveller/-q-a-n-t-u-n-i-e/
kwanyɛn
angle/-q-a-n-er-n/

kwanyɛn-anum
  pentagon/-q-a-n-er-n-a-n-u-m/
kwanyɛn-asia
  hexagon/-q-a-n-er-n-a-s-i-a/
kwanyɛn-du
  decagon/-q-a-n-er-n-d-u/
kwanyɛn-kron
  nonagon/-q-a-n-e-r-n-k-r-o-n/
kwanyɛn-nan
  rectangle/-q-a-n-er-n-n-a-n/
kwanyɛn-sa
  triangle/-q-a-n-er-n-s-a/
kwanyɛn-suon
  heptagon/-q-a-n-er-n-s-u-o-n/
kwanyɛn-twe
  octagon/-q-a-n-er-n-t-w-e/
kwasea
  fool/-q-a-s-e-a/
kwaseade
  foolishness/-q-a-s-e-a-d-e/
Kwasi
  Kwesi/k-w-a-s-i/
Kwasida
  Sunday/k-w-a-s-i-d-a/
kwata
  leprosy/-q-a-t-a/
kwatanyi
  leper/-q-a-t-a-n-i/
kwatiri
  avoid/-q-a-t-i-r-i/
Kwaw
  Kow/k-w-a-w/
ky

ch/-ch/
kyapem
  captain/-ch-a-p-e-m/
kye
  catch/-ch-e/
Kyead
  Chad/k-y-e-a-d/
Kyeadnyi
  Chadian/k-y-e-a-d-n-i/
Kyeaena
  China/k-y-e-a-e-n-a/
Kyeaenanyi
  Chinese/k-y-e-a-e-n-a-n-i/
kyeagye
  charge/-ch-e-a-j-e/
kyeale wote
  slippers/-ch-e-a-l-e -w-o-t-e/
kyeame
  spokesperson/-ch-e-a-m-e/
kyedɛ
  unless/-ch-e-d-er/
kyehoma
  rope/-c-h-e-h-o-m-a/
kyekyere
  tie/-ch-e-ch-e-r-e/
kyekyeretenyi
  miser/-ch-e-ch-e-r-e-t-e-n-i/
kyembiri
  cobra/-ch-e-m-m-i-r-i/
kyenam
  fried-fish/-ch-e-n-a-m/
kyenan
  spoor/-ch-e-n-a-n/

kyene
drum/-ch-e-n-e/
kyere
squeeze/-ch-e-r-e/
kyerɛ
train/-ch-e-r-e-r/
kyerɛ
teach/-ch-e-r-e-r/
kyerɛ
show/-ch-e-r-e-r/
kyerɛ ... ase
explain/-ch-e-r-e-r ... -a-s-e/
kyerɛ ... mu
translate/-ch-e-r-e-r ... -m-u/
kyerɛkyerɛnyi
professor/-ch-e-r-e-r-ch-e-r-e-r-n-i/
kyerɛma
drummer/-ch-e-r-e-r-m-a/
kyerɛpɛn
row/-ch-e-r-e-r-p-e-r-n/
kyerɛsɛ
mean/-ch-e-r-e-r-s-e-r/
kyerɛw
write/-ch-e-r-e-r-w/
kyerɛwdua
pen/-ch-e-r-e-r-w-d-u-a/
kyerɛwnyi
author/-ch-e-r-e-r-w-n-i/
kyerɛwsɛm
scripture/-ch-e-r-e-r-w-s-e-r-m/
kyew
fry/-ch-e-w/

kyeɔkɔlete
chocolate/-ch-e-or-k-or-l-e-t-e/
kyɛ
share/-ch-er/
kyɛ ... mu
divide/-ch-er ... -m-u/
kyɛfa
share/-ch-er-f-a/
kyɛfo
tarantula/-ch-er-f-o/
kyɛke
cheque/-ch-er-k-e/
kyɛkuw
category/-ch-er-k-u-w/
kyɛm
shield/-ch-er-m/
kyɛmu
fraction/-ch-er-m-u/
kyɛn
surpass/-ch-er-n/
kyɛn
than/-ch-er-n/
kyɛnse
pan/-ch-er-n-s-e/
kyɛr
delay/-ch-e-r-r/
kyɛw
hat/-ch-er-w/
kyia
greet/-ch-i-a/
kyigyinanyi
sponsor/-ch-i-j-i-n-a-n-i/
kyiis

cheese/-ch-i-i-s/
kyiita
cheetah/-ch-i-i-t-a/
kyikyi
telescope/-ch-i-ch-i/
kyikyiikyi
turbulent/-ch-i-ch-i-i-ch-i/
kyim
argument/-ch-i-m/
kyim
twist/-ch-i-m/
kyima
roam/-ch-i-m-a/
kyin ... mu
wring/-ch-i-n ... -m-u/
kyinkyinga
khebab/-ch-i-n-ch-i-n-g-a/
kyiri
hate/-ch-i-r-i/
kyiribra
teenage pregnancy/-ch-i-r-i-b-r-a/
kyiritaanyi
supporter/-ch-i-r-i-t-a-a-n-i/
l
l/-l/
labo
laboratory/-l-a-b-o/
Laeberia
Liberia/l-a-e-b-e-r-i-a/
Laeberianyi
Liberian/l-a-e-b-e-r-i-a-n-i/
Lakzembɔg

Luxembourg/l-a-kz-e-m-m-or-g/
Lakzembɔgnyi
Luxembourger/l-a-kz-e-m-m-or-g-n-i/
Laos
Laos/l-a-o-s/
Laosnyi
Lao/l-a-o-s-n-i/
laptop
laptop/-l-a-p-t-o-p/
leeti
late/-l-e-e-t-i/
lefte
lift/-l-e-f-t-e/
lenke
link/-l-e-n-k-e/
Lɛbanɔn
Lebanon/l-er-b-a-n-or-n/
Lɛbanɔnnyi
Lebanese/l-er-b-a-n-or-n-n-i/
Lɛndɛn
London/l-er-n-n-er-n/
lɛnse
lens/-l-er-n-s-e/
lɛtɛ
letter/-l-er-t-er/
Libia
Libya/l-i-b-i-a/
Libianyi
Libyan/l-i-b-i-a-n-i/
Lingala
Lingala/-l-i-n-g-a-l-a/
Lisooto

Lesotho/l-i-s-o-o-t-o/
Lisootonyi
Mosotho/l-i-s-o-o-t-o-n-i-e/
litiyɔm
lithium/-l-i-t-i-y-or-m/
logo
logo/-l-o-g-o/
lɔk
luck/-l-or-k/
lɔki
lucky/-l-or-k-i/
lɔre
lorry/-l-o-r-r-e/
Luganda
Luganda/l-u-g-a-n-n-a/
Luwo
Luwo/l-u-w-o/
m
m/-m/
ma
give/-m-a/
ma
let/-m-a/
ma
full/-m-a/
ma ...
for/-m-a .../
ma ... do
lift/-m-a ... -d-o/
ma ... kwan
allow/-m-a ... -q-a-n/
Maa
Maasai/m-a-a/

maame
mother/-m-a-a-m-e/
Madagaska
Madagascar/m-a-d-a-g-a-s-k-a/
magazin
magazine/-m-a-g-az-i-n/
maginisiyɔm
magnesium/-m-a-g-i-n-i-s-i-y-or-m/
Malabo-Gini
Equatorial Guinea/m-a-l-a-b-o-g-i-n-i/
Malagasi
Malagasy/m-a-l-a-g-a-s-i/
Malawi
Malawi/m-a-l-a-w-i/
Malawinyi
Malawian/m-a-l-a-w-i-n-i/
Maldivs
Maldives/m-a-l-d-i-v-s/
Maldivsnyi
Maldivian/m-a-l-d-i-v-s-n-i/
Malehyia
Malaysia/m-a-l-e-sh-i-a/
Malehyianyi
Malaysian/m-a-l-e-sh-i-a-n-i/
Mali
Mali/m-a-l-i/
mali-kraman
wolf/-m-a-l-i-k-r-a-m-a-n/
Malinyi
Malian/m-a-l-i-n-i/
mamba

citizen/-m-a-m-m-a/
mambɔenyi
traitor/-m-a-m-m-or-e-n-i/
mamforanyi
immigrant/-m-a-m-f-o-r-a-n-i/
mampam
alligator/-m-a-m-p-a-m/
man
nation/-m-a-n/
man
country/-m-a-n/
Manding
Manding/m-a-n-n-i-n-g/
mane
branch/-m-a-n-e/
manegya
manager/-m-a-n-e-j-a/
mango
mango/-m-a-n-g-o/
mangow
class/-m-a-n-g-o-w/
mankani
cocoyam/-m-a-n-k-a-n-i/
mankrado
vice-president/-m-a-n-k-r-a-d-o/
mansin
district/-m-a-n-s-i-n/
manso
litigation/-m-a-n-s-o/
mansotwenyi
litigant/-m-a-n-s-o-t-w-e-n-i/
mantaw
region/-m-a-n-t-a-w/

manyamanya
chaotic/-m-a-n-a-m-a-n-a/
manyina
national/-m-a-n-i-n-a/
mapa
pure/-m-a-p-a/
mape
map/-m-a-p-e/
masae-pɔnkɔ
zebra/-m-a-s-a-e-p-or-n-k-or/
Mateo
Matthew/m-a-t-e-o/
Mayanma
Myanmar/-m-a-y-a-n-m-a/
Mayanmanyi
Myanma/-m-a-y-a-n-m-a-n-i/
mbae
coming/-m-m-a-e/
mbaemu
extension/-m-m-a-e-m-u/
mbafoberemu
childhood/-m-m-a-f-o-b-e-r-e-m-u/
mbara
rule/-m-m-a-r-a/
mbara
law/-m-m-a-r-a/
mbasanten
generation/-m-m-a-s-a-n-t-e-n/
mbasu
springwater/-m-m-a-s-u/
mbeamudua
cross/-m-m-e-a-m-u-d-u-a/

mberantebere
youth/-m-m-e-r-a-n-t-e-b-e-r-e/
mbere
time/-m-m-e-r-e/
mberenhyehyɛe
timetable/-m-m-e-r-e-n-sh-e-sh-e-r-e/
mberesanten
eternity/-m-m-e-r-e-s-a-n-t-e-n/
mberɛ
flexible/-m-m-e-r-e-r/
Mbɛbusɛm
Proverbs/-m-b-er-b-u-s-er-m/
mbɛnsuon
frond/-m-m-er-n-s-u-o-n/
mbire
mushroom/-m-m-i-r-e/
mbirika
race/-m-m-i-r-i-k-a/
mbo
congratulations/-m-m-o/
mboa
aid/-m-m-o-a/
mboaba
bribe/-m-m-o-a-b-a/
mbobakan
calculus/-m-m-o-b-a-s-a-n-t-e-t-w-i/
mboframba
children/-m-m-a/
mbogya
blood/-m-m-o-j-a/
mbogyatu

bleeding/-m-m-o-j-a-t-u/
mbom
except that/-m-m-o-m/
mborɔnsa
rum/-m-m-o-r-o-r-n-s-a/
mbɔbɔr
pitiful/-m-m-o-r-b-o-r-r/
mbɔbɔrwa
pitiable/-m-m-o-r-b-o-r-r-w-a/
mbɔdembɔ
achievement/-m-m-or-d-e-m-m-or/
mbɔden
effort/-m-m-or-d-e-n/
mbɔho
multiplication/-m-m-or-h-o/
mbɔre
dough/-m-m-o-r-r-e/
mbɔtohɔ
procrastination/-m-m-or-t-o-h-or/
mbrahyɛbagua
parliament/-m-m-r-a-sh-e-r-b-a-g-u-a/
mbrɛ
as/-m-m-r-e-r/
mbrɛw
weak/-m-m-r-e-r-w/
mbrɛwyɛ
weakness/-m-m-r-e-r-w-y-e-r/
mbuada
fasting/-m-m-u-a-d-a/
mbuae

answer/-m-m-u-a-e/
mbubui
 paraliesis/-m-m-u-b-u-i/
mbuwado
 lid/-m-m-u-w-a-d-o/
me
 my/-m-e/
me
 me/-m-e/
me
 I/-m-e/
me afe wo
 i miss you/-m-e -a-f-e -w-o/
me da wo ase
 thank you/-m-e -d-a -w-o -a-s-e/
me ma wo adwe
 good evening/-m-e -m-a -w-o -a-d-w-e/
me ma wo aha
 good afternoon/-m-e -m-a -w-o -a-h-a/
me ma wo akye
 good morning/-m-e -m-a -w-o -a-ch-e/
me pa wo kyɛw
 please/-m-e -p-a -w-o -ch-er-w/
medaase
 thanks/-m-e-d-a-a-s-e/
mede
 mine/-m-e-d-e/
mee
 be satisfied/-m-e-e/
meho

 myself/-m-e-h-o/
mel
 mail/-m-e-l/
mem
 sink/-m-e-m/
memem
 drown/-m-e-m-e-m/
Memeneda
 Saturday/-m-e-m-e-n-e-d-a/
mena
 broom/-m-e-n-a/
menaba
 broomstick/-m-e-n-a-b-a/
mene
 swallow/-m-e-n-e/
mene
 throat/-m-e-n-e/
merekye
 milk/-m-e-r-e-ch-e/
mesia
 messiah/-m-e-s-i-a/
metinyi
 bus conductor/-m-e-t-i-n-i/
mɛtafɔ
 metaphor/-m-er-t-a-f-or/
mfaso
 profit/-m-f-a-s-o/
mfatoho
 example/-m-f-a-t-o-h-o/
mfedu
 decade/-m-f-e-d-u/
mfeha
 century/-m-f-e-h-a/

mfemfem
moustache/-m-f-e-m-f-e-m/
mfɛfo
age group/-m-f-er-f-o/
mfoba
pimple/-m-f-o-b-a/
mfomso
mistake/-m-f-o-m-s-o/
mfonyin
image/-m-f-o-n-i-n/
mfonyiwaa
thumbnail/-m-f-o-n-i-w-a-a/
mfɔte
termite/-m-f-or-t-e/
mframa
wind/-m-f-r-a-m-a/
mframamframa
windy/-m-f-r-a-m-a-m-f-r-a-m-a/
mfuruma
belly button/-m-f-u-r-u-m-a/
mfutuw
dust/-m-f-u-t-u-w/
mfuw
foliage/-m-f-u-w/
mia
press/-m-i-a/
minisitiri
ministry/-m-i-n-i-s-i-t-i-r-i/
Misrim
Egypt/-m-i-s-r-i-m/
Misrimnyi
Egyptian/-m-i-s-r-i-m-n-i/
mita

metre/-m-i-t-a/
mmɔbɔ-mmɔbɔ
sad/-m-m-or-b-or-m-m-or-b-or/
moho
yourselves/-m-o-h-o/
moma
forehead/-m-o-m-a/
mona
deliver/-m-o-n-a/
mono
fresh/-m-o-n-o/
moo
rice/-m-o-o/
Moroko
Morocco/m-o-r-o-k-o/
Morokonyi
Moroccan/m-o-r-o-k-o-n-i-e/
moskoveyɔm
Moscovium/-m-o-s-k-o-v-e-y-or-m/
moto
motorbike/-m-o-t-o/
Mozambik
Mozambique/-m-oz-a-m-m-i-k/
Mozambiknyi
Mozambican/-m-oz-a-m-m-i-k-n-i/
mɔmɔe
stinking fish seasoning/-m-or-m-or-e/
Mɔngolia
Mongolia/m-or-n-g-o-l-i-a/
Mɔngolianyi

Mongolian/*m-or-n-g-o-l-i-a-n-i*/

mɔnita
monitor/*-m-or-n-i-t-a*/

Mɔrihyiɔs
Mauritius/*m-o-r-r-i-sh-i-o-r-s*/

Mɔrihyiɔsnyi
Mauritian/*m-o-r-r-i-sh-i-o-r-s-n-i*/

Mɔritaniya
Mauritania/*m-o-r-r-i-t-a-n-i-y-a*/

Mɔritaniyanyi
Mauritanian/*m-o-r-r-i-t-a-n-i-y-a-n-i*/

mpa
bed/*-m-p-a*/

mpaa
curse/*-m-p-a-a*/

mpadua
bedstead/*-m-p-a-d-u-a*/

mpae
prayer/*-m-p-a-e*/

mpampa
pap/*-m-p-a-m-p-a*/

mpamugoro
sex/*-m-p-a-m-u-g-o-r-o*/

mpasar
stroll/*-m-p-a-s-a-r*/

mpe
sleep crust/*-m-p-e*/

mpempem
thousands/*-m-p-e-m-p-e-m*/

mpena
concubine/*-m-p-e-n-a*/

mpena
boyfriend/*-m-p-e-n-a*/

mpenatwe
courtship/*-m-p-e-n-a-t-w-e*/

mpɛmpɛnso
milestone/*-m-p-er-m-p-er-n-s-o*/

mpɛn
times/*-m-p-er-n*/

mpoano
beach/*-m-p-o-a-n-o*/

mpoano
coast/*-m-p-o-a-n-o*/

mpontu
development/*-m-p-o-n-t-u*/

mpɔta
neighbourhood/*-m-p-or-t-a*/

mpɔtamunyi
neighbour/*-m-p-or-t-a-m-u-n-i-e*/

mpurkaa
bedbug/*-m-p-u-r-k-a-a*/

mpuw
threat/*-m-p-u-w*/

mu
inside/*-m-u*/

mu
in/*-m-u*/

mua
shut/*-m-u-a*/

mudɔ
depth/*-m-u-d-or*/

mumu
mute/*-m-u-m-u-o*/

Mumu
December/-m-u-m-u-o/
muna
cloud/-m-u-n-a/
mununkum
cloud/-m-u-n-u-n-k-u-m/
muo
be evil/-m-u-o/
muoko
pepper/-m-u-o-k-o/
musumunsum
cloudy/-m-u-s-u-m-u-n-s-u-m/
n
n/-n/
na
and/-n-a/
na
expensive/-n-a/
na
scarcity/-n-a/
na
scarce/-n-a/
naaso
but/-n-a-a-s-o/
naetrogyen
nitrogen/-n-a-e-t-r-o-j-e-n/
nam
meat/-n-a-m/
nam
pass by/-n-a-m/
Namibia
Namibia/n-a-m-i-b-i-a/
Namibianyi

Namibian/-n-a-m-i-b-i-a-n-i/
namɔn
footstep/-n-a-m-or-n/
nan
leg/-n-a-n/
nana
ancestor/-n-a-n-a/
nanabaa
grandma/-n-a-n-a-b-a-a/
nanabanyin
grandfather/-n-a-n-a-b-a-n-i-n/
nanaben
stranger/-n-a-n-a-b-e-n/
nanakansoa
great-grandchild/-n-a-n-a-s-a-
n-t-e -t-w-i-s-o-a/
nandwɛ
ankle/-n-a-n-n-w-er/
nane
melt/-n-a-n-e/
nanka
puff-adder/-n-a-n-k-a/
nansa
foot/-n-a-n-s-a/
nansoa
toe/-n-a-n-s-o-a/
nantenyi
pedestrian/-n-a-n-t-e-n-i/
nantew
walk/-n-a-n-t-e-w/
nanteyie
godspeed/-n-a-n-t-e-y-i-e/
nantiri

heel/-n-a-n-t-i-r-i/
nantu
 calf/-n-a-n-t-u/
nantwi
 cow/-n-a-n-t-w-i/
nantwinam
 beef/-n-a-n-t-w-i-n-a-m/
napken
 napkin/-n-a-p-k-e-n/
nara
 nara/-n-a-r-a/
ndaa
 grave/-n-n-a-a/
ndaadaa
 disappointment/-n-n-a-a-d-a-a/
ndaano
 the other time/-n-n-a-a-n-o/
ndaano
 the other day/-n-n-a-a-n-o/
ndaansayi
 nowadays/-n-n-a-a-n-s-a-y-i/
ndaase
 thanksgiving/-n-n-a-a-s-e/
ndaawɔtwe
 eight days/-n-n-a-a-w-or-t-w-e/
nde
 voice/-n-n-e/
ndebɔneyɛ
 vice/-n-n-e-b-or-n-e-y-er/
ndeda
 yesterday/-n-n-e-d-a/
ndeɛmba
 things/-n-n-e-er-m-m-a/

ndɛ
 today/-n-n-er/
ndinoa
 rights/-n-n-i-n-o-a/
ndɔbaa
 harvest/-n-n-or-b-a-a/
ndɔboa
 cooperation/-n-n-or-b-o-a/
ndɔboakuw
 team/-n-n-or-b-o-a-k-u-w/
ndua
 wood/-n-n-u-a/
nduamu
 entry/-n-n-u-a-m-u/
ndwom
 music/-n-n-w-o-m/
ndwom
 song/-n-n-w-o-m/
ndwomtow
 singing/-n-n-w-o-m-t-o-w/
ne
 his/-n-e/
ne
 her/-n-e/
ne
 of/-n-e/
ne
 its/-n-e/
nede
 his/-n-e-d-e/
nede
 hers/-n-e-d-e/
neho

himself/-n-e-h-o/

nenam
walk about/-n-e-n-a-m/

Nepɔl
Nepal/n-e-p-or-l/

Nepɔlnyi
Nepali/-n-e-p-or-l-n-i/

neyɔn
neon/-n-e-y-or-n/

nɛɛse
nurse/-n-er-er-s-e/

nɛɛvɔs
nervous/-n-er-er-v-or-s/

nɛtewɛke
network/-n-er-t-e-w-er-k-e/

ngaa
waah/-n-g-a-a/

ngo
oil/-n-g-o/

ngyeso
response/-n-j-e-s-o/

ngyetomu
acceptance/-n-j-e-t-o-m-u-o/

Ngyiresi
England/n-j-i-r-e-s-i/

nhwehwɛmu
investigation/-n-h-w-e-h-w-er-m-u/

nhyiamu
meeting/-n-sh-i-a-m-u/

nhyira
blessing/-n-sh-i-r-a/

nhyiren

flower/-n-sh-i-r-e-n/

nhyɛ
command/-n-sh-er/

nhyɛananmu
replacement/-n-sh-er-a-n-a-n-m-u/

nibima
cryptolepis sanguinolenta/-n-i-b-i-m-a/

Nigyɛɛ
Niger/n-i-j-er-er/

Nigyɛɛnyi
Nigerien/-n-i-j-er-er-n-i/

nihoneyɔm
Nihonium/-n-i-h-o-n-e-y-or-m/

nika
shorts/-n-i-k-a/

nino
siren/-n-i-n-o/

niwklɔs
nucleus/-n-i-w-k-l-or-s/

niwtrɔn
neutron/-n-i-w-t-r-o-r-n/

nka
smell/-n-k-a/

nkaano
ancient times/-n-k-a-a-n-o/

nkabomkuw
union/-n-k-a-b-o-m-k-u-w/

nkae
memory/-n-k-a-e/

nkae
remainder/-n-k-a-e/

nkakrankakra
little by little/-n-k-a-k-r-a-n-k-a-k-r-a/
nkate
groundnut/-n-k-a-t-e/
nkenyan
revival/-n-k-e-n-y-a-n/
nketenkete
pins and needles/-n-k-e-t-e-n-k-e-t-e/
nkɛntɛnso
influence/-n-k-er-n-t-er-n-s-o/
nko
only/-n-k-o/
nko
alone/-n-k-o/
nkoasom
servanthood/-n-k-o-a-s-o-m/
nkodwobo
manganese/-n-k-o-d-w-o-b-o/
nkogu
defeat/-n-k-o-g-u-o/
nkokoamu
privately/-n-k-o-k-o-a-m-u/
nkontaa
accounts/-n-k-o-n-t-a-a/
nkontaabu
mathematics/-n-k-o-n-t-a-a-b-u/
nkontaabu
computing/-n-k-o-n-t-a-a-b-u/
nkonyaa
trick/-n-k-o-n-y-a-a/
nkonyim

victory/-n-k-o-n-i-m/
nkorokoro
one by one/-n-k-o-r-o-k-o-r-o/
nkorɔfo
people/-n-k-o-r-o-r-f-o/
nkɔn
disgusting/-n-k-or-n/
nkɔsan
trip/-n-k-or-s-a-n/
nkɔso
improvement/-n-k-or-s-o/
nkra
bye/-n-k-r-a/
nkra
message/-n-k-r-a/
nkrabea
destiny/-n-k-r-a-b-e-a/
nkramodan
mosque/-n-k-r-a-m-o-d-a-n/
Nkran
Accra/-n-k-r-a-n/
nkran
ants/-n-k-r-a-n/
nkrandaa
verandah/-n-k-r-a-n-n-a-a/
Nkrankasa
GaDangme/-n-k-r-a-n-k-a-s-a/
nkrumsi
sighing/-n-k-r-u-m-s-i/
nkrɔm
snoring/-n-k-r-o-r-m/
nku
sheabutter/-n-k-u/

nkukunkaka
junk/-n-k-u-k-u-n-k-a-k-a/
nkunuma
okra/-n-k-u-n-u-m-a/
nkunyimdinyi
victor/-n-k-u-n-i-m-d-i-n-i/
nkuranhyɛ
encouragement/-n-k-u-r-a-n-sh-e-r/
nkuto
pomade/-n-k-u-t-o/
nkwa
vitality/-n-q-a/
nkwaba
fish-hook/-n-q-a-b-a/
nkwabambɔ
safety/-n-q-a-b-a-m-m-or/
nkwagye
salvation/-n-q-a-j-e/
nkwan
soup/-n-q-a-n/
nkwanta
intersection/-n-q-a-n-t-a/
nkwantabisa
signpost/-n-q-a-n-t-a-b-i-s-a/
nkwantia
outskirt/-n-q-a-n-t-i-a/
nkwaseasɛm
folly/-n-q-a-s-e-a-s-er-m/
nkwaseasɛm
nonsense/-n-q-a-s-e-a-s-er-m/
nkyekyɛmu
division/-n-ch-e-ch-er-m-u/

nkyekyɛmu
verse/-n-ch-e-ch-er-m-u/
nkyene
salt/-n-ch-e-n-e/
nkyerɛase
explanation/-n-ch-e-r-e-r-a-s-e/
nkyerɛkyerɛmu
definition/-n-ch-e-r-e-r-ch-e-r-e-r-m-u/
nkyerɛmu
meaning/-n-ch-e-r-e-r-m-u/
nkyetɔn
kidnapping/-n-ch-e-t-or-n/
nkyia
greeting/-n-ch-i-a/
nkyidɔm
rearguard/-n-ch-i-d-or-m/
nkyɛkyɛre
grass/-n-ch-e-r-ch-e-r-r-e/
nna
then/-n-n-a/
nnoboa
cooperative/-n-n-o-b-o-a/
nnuho
repentance/-n-n-u-h-o/
nnyi
not have/-n-n-i/
no
her/-n-o/
no
him/-n-o/
no
the/-n-o/

noa
  cook/-n-o-a/
noho
  other side/-n-o-h-o/
nokware
  truth/-n-o-q-a-r-e/
nom
  drink/-n-o-m/
Nowa
  Noah/n-o-w-a/
nsa
  hand/-n-s-a/
nsa
  liquor/-n-s-a/
nsa-awerɛwba
  fingernail/-n-s-a-a-w-e-r-e-r-w-b-a/
nsaamaa
  maggot/-n-s-a-a-m-a-a/
nsaano
  fingertip/-n-s-a-a-n-o/
nsabow
  drunkenness/-n-s-a-b-o-w/
nsabran
  appellation/-n-s-a-b-r-a-n/
nsaefuw
  palmwine/-n-s-a-e-f-u-w/
nsah
  alcohol/-n-s-a-h/
nsamanwa
  tuberculosis/-n-s-a-m-a-n-w-a/
nsatea
  finger/-n-s-a-t-e-a/

nsaterɛ
  palm/-n-s-a-t-e-r-e-r/
nsensansensan
  striped/-n-s-e-n-s-a-n-s-e-n-s-a-n/
nsesa
  change/-n-s-e-s-a/
nsesatumi
  impact/-n-s-e-s-a-t-u-m-i-e/
nsew
  oath/-n-s-e-w/
nsiho
  interest/-n-s-i-h-o/
nso
  ash/-n-s-o/
nso
  yet/-n-s-o/
nsɔe
  thorn/-n-s-or-e/
nsɔhwɛ
  assessment/-n-s-or-h-w-er/
nsɔhwɛ
  exam/-n-s-or-h-w-er/
nsrahwɛ
  tour/-n-s-r-a-h-w-e-r/
nsu
  water/-n-s-u/
nsu-akyekyerɛ
  turtle/-n-s-u-a-ch-e-ch-e-r-e-r/
nsuadehɛn
  submarine/-n-s-u-a-d-e-h-er-n/
nsuban
  dam/-n-s-u-b-a-n/
nsukyerɛma

snow/-n-s-u-ch-e-r-e-r-m-a/

nsukɔm
thirst/-n-s-u-k-or-m/

nsunam
fish/-n-s-u-n-a-m/

nsunsu
liquid/-n-s-u-n-s-u/

nsusono
hippopotamus/-n-s-u-s-o-n-o/

nsusui
measure/-n-s-u-s-u-i/

nsutae
lake/-n-s-u-t-a-e/

nsutene
river/-n-s-u-t-e-n-e/

nsutɔ
rain/-n-s-u-t-or/

nsutɔbere
rainy season/-n-s-u-t-o-r-b-e-r-e/

nsuyiri
flood/-n-s-u-y-i-r-i/

ntafi
spittle/-n-t-a-f-i/

ntafo
twins/-n-t-a-f-o/

ntama
cloth/-n-t-a-m-a/

ntamu
among/-n-t-a-m-u/

ntansa
triplets/-n-t-a-n-s-a/

ntare

clothes/-n-t-a-r-e/

ntawantawa
controversy/-n-t-a-w-a-n-t-a-w-a/

ntentan
web/-n-t-e-n-t-a-n/

ntɛ
spin-top/-n-t-er/

ntɛ
spinning top/-n-t-er/

ntɛm
quick/-n-t-er-m/

ntɛm
fast/-n-t-er-m/

ntɛm
early/-n-t-er-m/

nti
so/-n-t-i/

ntini
vein/-n-t-i-n-i/

ntini
root/-n-t-i-n-i/

ntoboa
offering/-n-t-o-b-o-a/

ntoburo
measles/-n-t-o-b-u-r-o/

ntodo
addition/-n-t-o-d-o/

ntokowantokowa
brown/-n-t-o-k-o-w-a-n-t-o-k-o-w-a/

ntoma
fabric/-n-t-o-m-a/

ntomagow
 rag/-n-t-o-m-a-g-o-w/
ntontom
 mosquito/-n-t-o-n-t-o-m/
ntonton
 exultation/-n-t-o-n-t-o-n/
ntos
 tomato/-n-t-o-s/
ntoso
 bonus/-n-t-o-s-o/
ntoto
 discord/-n-t-o-t-o/
ntɔhwɛ
 testis/-n-t-or-h-w-er/
ntropo
 eggplant/-n-t-r-o-p-o/
ntrɔba
 garden egg/-n-t-r-o-r-b-a/
ntui
 porpoise/-n-t-u-i/
ntuntu
 caterpillar/-n-t-u-n-t-u/
nu
 immerse/-n-u/
nu ... ho
 repent/-n-u ... -h-o/
nu ... hu
 regret/-n-u ... -h-u/
nua
 cousin/-n-u-a/
nua
 sibling/-n-u-a/
nua-banyin
 brother/-n-u-a-b-a-n-i-n/
nuhu
 regret/-n-u-h-u-o/
num
 suckle/-n-u-m/
numfo
 breast/-n-u-m-f-o/
numfonsu
 breastmilk/-n-u-m-f-o-n-s-u/
numfuano
 nipple/-n-u-m-f-u-a-n-o/
nunu
 stir/-n-u-n-u-o/
nunum
 mint/-n-u-n-u-m/
nwa
 snail/-n-w-a/
nwanwa
 amazing/-n-w-a-n-w-a/
nwanwa
 wonder/-n-w-a-n-w-a/
nwewe
 sweetheart/-n-w-e-w-e/
nwewee
 rheumatism/-n-w-e-w-e-e/
nwin
 cold/-n-w-i-n/
nwomakorabea
 library/-n-w-o-m-a-k-o-r-a-b-e-a/
nwomasua
 education/-n-w-o-m-a-s-u-a/
nya
 gain/-n-y-a/

nyaatwem
hypocrisy/-n-y-a-a-t-w-e-m/
nyam
grind/-n-y-a-m/
nyame
god/-n-y-a-m-e/
nyan
wake up/-n-y-a-n/
nyan
wake/-n-y-a-n/
nyane
awaken/-n-y-a-n-e/
nyankoma-ketebowa
scorpion/-n-y-a-n-k-o-m-a-k-e-t-e-b-o-w-a/
nyankontɔn
rainbow/-n-y-a-n-k-o-n-t-or-n/
Nyankopɔn
Almighty/-n-y-a-n-k-o-p-or-n/
nyansa
wisdom/-n-y-a-n-s-a/
nyansahobrɛase
prudence/-n-y-a-n-s-a-h-o-b-r-e-r-a-s-e/
nyansahobrɛaseno
prudent/-n-y-a-n-s-a-h-o-b-r-e-r-a-s-e-n-o/
nyansanyansa
cunning/-n-y-a-n-s-a-n-a-n-s-a/
nyansanyansa
wise/-n-y-a-n-s-a-n-a-n-s-a/
nyansanyi
savant/-n-y-a-n-s-a-n-i/

nyansapɛ
philosophy/-n-y-a-n-s-a-p-er/
nyansapɛnyi
philosopher/-n-y-a-n-s-a-p-er-n-i/
nye
with/-n-y-e/
nye
defecate/-n-y-e/
nyee
shit/-n-y-e-e/
nyena
firewood/-n-y-e-n-a/
nyepi
jaw/-n-y-e-p-i/
nyɛe
verb/-n-y-er-e/
nyɛe
action/-n-y-er-e/
nyɛetamsi
adverb/-n-y-er-e-t-a-m-s-i/
nyɛn
rear/-n-y-er-n/
nyi
person/-n-i/
nyi
this/-n-i/
nyiano
information/-n-i-a-n-o/
nyianyim
introduction/-n-i-a-n-i-m/
nyianyim
preface/-n-i-a-n-i-m/

nyifa
right/-n-i-f-a/
nyifimu
subtraction/-n-i-f-i-m-u/
nyim
success/-n-i-m/
nyim
know/-n-i-m/
nyimdee
knowledge/-n-i-m-d-e-e/
nyimfe
age/-n-i-m-f-e/
nyimpa
being/-n-i-m-p-a/
nyin
age/-n-i-n/
nyin
billy/-n-i-n/
nyina
all/-n-i-n-a/
nyinaa
entire/-n-i-n-a-a/
nyinara
total/-n-i-n-a-r-a/
nyinara
all/-n-i-n-a-r-a/
nyini
growth/-n-i-n-i/
nyinkyɛre
longevity/-n-i-n-ch-e-r-r-e/
nyinsɛn
pregnancy/-n-i-n-s-er-n/
nyinsɛn

be pregnant/-n-i-n-s-er-n/
nyinyande
torture/-n-i-n-y-a-n-n-e/
nyiyiano
impertinence/-n-i-y-i-a-n-o/
nyiyimu
favouritism/-n-i-y-i-m-u/
nyo
mass/-n-y-o/
o
oa/-o/
o
emphasis/-o/
obi
somebody/-o-b-i-e/
obiara
everyone/-o-b-i-a-r-a/
obiara-amambu
democracy/-o-b-i-a-r-a-a-m-a-m-
m-u/
obibiara
each and everyone/-o-b-i-b-i-
a-r-a/
Obubuo
November/-o-b-u-b-u-o/
oganeson
Oganesson/-o-g-a-n-e-s-o-n/
Olimpek
Olympics/-o-l-i-m-p-e-k/
Oman
Oman/-o-m-a-n/
Omannyi
Omani/-o-m-a-n-n-i/

onyin
  python/-o-n-i-n/
osuanyi
  disciple/-o-s-u-a-n-i/
owu
  death/-o-w-u-o/
owura
  sir/-o-w-u-r-a/
owurayere
  missus/-o-w-u-r-a-y-e-r-e/
oyiwa
  so there/-o-y-i-w-a/
ɔ
  he/-or/
ɔ
  she/-or/
ɔ
  aw/-or/
ɔberan
  strong/-o-r-b-e-r-a-n/
ɔbrafo
  executioner/-o-r-b-r-a-f-o/
ɔdomankoma
  almighty/-o-r-d-o-m-a-n-k-o-m-a/
ɔdɔ
  dear/-or-d-or/
ɔfese
  office/-or-f-e-s-e/
ɔha
  hundred/-or-h-a/
ɔhenebabea
  princess/-or-h-e-n-e-b-a-b-e-a/
ɔhenebanyin

  prince/-or-h-e-n-e-b-a-n-i-n/
ɔkorow
  boat/-o-r-k-o-r-o-w/
ɔkɔre
  eagle/-o-r-k-o-r-r-e/
ɔksegyen
  oxygen/-or-k-s-e-j-e-n/
ɔksegyen
  oxygen/-or-k-s-e-j-e-n/
ɔkye
  brook/-or-ch-e/
ɔkyena
  tomorrow/-or-ch-e-n-a/
Ɔlgyeria
  Algeria/ɔ-l-j-e-r-i-a/
ɔmampanyin
  president/-or-m-a-m-p-a-n-i-n/
ɔno
  that person/-n-i -d-er-m/
ɔpepem
  million/-or-p-e-p-e-m/
ɔpepem-apem
  billion/-or-p-e-p-e-m-a-p-e-m/
ɔpepem-ɔpepem
  trillion/-or-p-e-p-e-m-or-p-e-p-e-m/
Ɔpɛ
  dry season/ɔ-p-er/
Ɔpɛpɔn
  January/-or-p-er-p-or-n/
ɔrengye
  orange/-o-r-r-e-n-j-e/
ɔsɔ

fox/-or-s-or/

Ɔstreliya
Australia/ɔ-s-t-r-e-l-i-y-a/

ɔtisim
autism/-or-t-i-s-i-m/

ɔtwe
antelope/-or-t-w-e/

ɔtwea
serves you right/-or-t-w-e-a/

ɔware
oware/-o-r-w-a-r-e/

ɔyɛadeyie
fixer/-or-y-er-a-d-e-y-i-e/

p
p/-p/

pa
good/-p-a/

paa
very/-p-a-a/

paado
outside/-p-a-a-d-o/

paake
park/-p-a-a-k-e/

paam
plan/-p-a-a-m/

paasole
parsley/-p-a-a-s-o-l-e/

pade
option/-p-a-d-e/

padi
partner/-p-a-d-i/

pae ... mu
split/-p-a-e ... -m-u/

paepe
tap/-p-a-e-p-e/

pagya
lift up/-p-a-j-a/

pagya
raise/-p-a-j-a/

pah
rump/-p-a-h/

Pakestan
Pakistan/p-a-k-e-s-t-a-n/

Pakestannyi
Pakistani/p-a-k-e-s-t-a-n-n-i/

Palestaen
Palestine/p-a-l-e-s-t-a-e-n/

Palestaennyi
Palestinean/p-a-l-e-s-t-a-e-n-n-i/

pam
sew/-p-a-m/

pamsam
tattered/-p-a-m-s-a-m/

pan
bat/-p-a-n/

pande
injection/-p-a-n-n-e/

panyin
elder/-p-a-n-i-n/

panyin
adult/-p-a-n-i-n/

papa
good/-p-a-p-a/

papaah
fan/-p-a-p-a-a-h/

papaapa

very much/-p-a-p-a-a-p-a/

papayɛ
virtue/-p-a-p-a-y-er/

pare
second/-p-a-r-e/

pasar
stroll/-p-a-s-a-r/

Pasefek
Pacific/p-a-s-e-f-e-k/

paspɔte
passport/-p-a-s-p-or-t-e/

pata
shade/-p-a-t-a/

pata
pacify/-p-a-t-a/

pata
hut/-p-a-t-a/

pataakowa
ant/-p-a-t-a-a-k-o-w-a/

pataku
hyena/-p-a-t-a-k-u/

patapaa
bullying/-p-a-t-a-p-a-a/

patapaanyi
bully/-p-a-t-a-p-a-a-n-i/

patu
owl/-p-a-t-u/

paye
pie/-p-a-y-e/

pea
spear/-p-e-a/

pefee
clearly/-p-e-f-e-e/

pem
bump into/-p-e-m/

pem
flow/-p-e-m/

pen
clear/-p-e-n/

pene
agree/-p-e-n-e/

penke
pink/-p-e-n-k-e/

penpen
frankly/-p-e-n-p-e-n/

pentoa
beaker/-p-e-n-t-o-a/

pepa
wipe/-p-e-p-a/

pepere
wriggle/-p-e-p-e-r-e/

pete
scatter/-p-e-t-e/

pɛ
want/-p-er/

pɛ
will/-p-er/

pɛ
perfect/-p-er/

pɛ
like/-p-er/

pɛe
chisl/-p-er-e/

pɛɛmen
perm/-p-er-er-m-e-n/

pɛnsere

pencil/-p-e-r-n-s-e-r-e/

pɛnyi
buyer/-p-er-n-i/

pɛpɛɛ
miserly/-p-er-p-er-er/

pɛr
same/-p-e-r-r/

pɛsewa
pesewa/-p-er-s-e-w-a/

pɛsɛmenkomenya
selfishness/-p-er-s-er-m-e-n-k-o-
m-e-n-y-a/

pɛtɛ
vulture/-p-er-t-er/

pia
bedroom/-p-i-a/

pia
push/-p-i-a/

pia
room/-p-i-a/

pieto
underwear/-p-i-e-t-o/

pii
many/-p-i-i/

pintinn
firmly/-p-i-n-t-i-n-n/

pira
injure/-p-i-r-a/

pirade
dangerous/-p-i-r-a-d-e/

pirahu
danger/-p-i-r-a-h-u/

pito

pito/-p-i-t-o/

piza
pizza/-p-iz-a/

planɛte
planet/-p-l-a-n-er-t-e/

plasta
plaster/-p-l-a-s-t-a/

plastek
plastic/-p-l-a-s-t-e-k/

po
sea/-p-o/

pohyɛn
ship/-p-o-sh-er-n/

pokyere
chain/-p-o-ch-e-r-e/

poliisi
police/-p-o-l-i-i-s-i/

poma
staff/-p-o-m-a/

pon
table/-p-o-n/

ponto
party/-p-o-n-t-o/

popo
tremble/-p-o-p-o/

posɔfese
post office/-p-o-s-or-f-e-s-e/

potaseyɔm
potassium/-p-o-t-a-s-e-y-or-m/

potumantu
suitcase/-p-o-t-u-m-a-n-t-u/

pow
reject/-p-o-w/

Powbere
Autumn/p-o-w-b-e-r-e/

pɔmpɔ
boil/-p-or-m-p-or/

pɔn
shut down/-p-or-n/

pɔn
major/-p-or-n/

pɔnkɔ
horse/-p-or-n-k-or/

pɔɔn
pound/-p-or-or-n/

pɔre
bleach/-p-o-r-r-e/

pɔtee
specific/-p-or-t-e-e/

pɔtɔɔ
utterly/-p-or-t-or-or/

pɔw
joint/-p-or-w/

pɔw
grove/-p-or-w/

pɔw
point/-p-or-w/

pɔw
knot/-p-or-w/

pra
sweep/-p-r-a/

prako
pig/-p-r-a-k-o/

prakoba
piglet/-p-r-a-k-o-b-a/

prakonam

pork/-p-r-a-k-o-n-a-m/

prakontwεre
pigfeet/-p-r-a-k-o-n-t-w-e-r-r-e/

prente
print/-p-r-e-n-t-e/

prεko
in advance/-p-r-e-r-k-o/

prεkopε
immediately/-p-r-e-r-k-o-p-e-r/

prεkεsε
Tetrapleura tetraptera/-p-r-e-r-k-e-r-s-e-r/

prεm
cannon/-p-r-e-r-m/

prεte
dish/-p-r-e-r-t-e/

protɔn
proton/-p-r-o-t-o-r-n/

prɔw
rot/-p-r-o-r-w/

prɔwyε
corruption/-p-r-o-r-w-y-e-r/

puei
exit/-p-u-e-i/

puei
log out/-p-u-e-i/

puow
bark/-p-u-o-w/

puti
poke/-p-u-t-i-e/

puw
belch/-p-u-w/

r

r/-r/
Rahyia
Russia/-r-a-sh-i-a/
Rahyianyi
Russian/-r-a-sh-i-a-n-i/
Reyuniɔn
Reunion/-r-e-y-u-n-i-or-n/
Romafo
Romans/-r-o-m-a-f-o/
roosu
rose/-r-o-o-s-u-o/
rɔkɛte
rocket/-r-o-r-k-e-r-t-e/
Rwanda
Rwanda/-r-w-a-n-n-a/
Rwandanyi
Rwandan/-r-w-a-n-n-a-n-i/
s
s/-s/
sa
heal/-s-a/
sa
battle/-s-a/
sa
enema/-s-a/
sa
deplete/-s-a/
saa
kidney/-s-a-a/
saa ara
normal/-s-a-a -a-r-a/
saadwe
infertile/-s-a-a-d-w-e/

saafee
key/-s-a-a-f-e-e/
saana
in fact/-s-a-a-n-a/
saekɔ
psychology/-s-a-e-k-or/
Saeprɔs
Cyprus/-s-a-e-p-r-o-r-s/
Saeprɔsnyi
Cypriot/-s-a-e-p-r-o-r-s-n-i/
Sahara Anee
Western Sahara/-s-a-h-a-r-a -a-n-e-e/
Sahara Aneenyi
Western Saharan/-s-a-h-a-r-a -a-n-e-e-n-i/
sakasaka
dishevelled/-s-a-k-a-s-a-k-a/
sakasaka
centipede/-s-a-k-a-s-a-k-a/
saman
ghost/-s-a-m-a-n/
saman
sue/-s-a-m-a-n/
samanade
hell/-s-a-m-a-n-a-d-e/
samina
soap/-s-a-m-i-n-a/
samunyi
journalist/-s-a-m-u-n-i-e/
san
return/-s-a-n/
sane

infect/-s-a-n-e/

sanku
guitar/-s-a-n-k-u/

santene
procession/-s-a-n-t-e-n-e/

santom
sweet potato/-s-a-n-t-o-m/

Sao Tome na Prensepe
Sao Tome and Principe/-s-a-o
t-o-m-e -n-a -p-r-e-n-s-e-p-e/

Sao Tome na Prensepenyi
Santomean/-s-a-o t-o-m-e -n-a -
p-r-e-n-s-e-p-e-n-i/

sapɔw
sponge/-s-a-p-or-w/

sare
desert/-s-a-r-e/

saspan
saucepan/-s-a-s-p-a-n/

satwanyi
pioneer/-s-a-t-w-a-n-i/

saw
dance/-s-a-w/

saw
scoop/-s-a-w/

Sawdi Arabia
Saudi Arabia/-s-a-w-d-i -a-r-a-b-
i-a/

Sawdi Arabianyi
Saudi Arabian/s-a-w-d-i -a-r-a-
b-i-a-n-i/

sayense
science/-s-a-y-e-n-s-e/

se
tooth/-s-e/

se
say/-s-e/

se ... pɛ
ask ... out/-s-e ... -p-er/

seadeyɛ
able/-s-e-a-d-e-y-er/

sebɔ
leopard/-s-e-b-or/

sedua
toothbrush/-s-e-d-u-a/

seduru
toothpaste/-s-e-d-u-r-u-o/

Sehyɛls
Seychelles/-s-e-sh-er-l-s/

Sehyɛlsnyi
Seselwa/-s-e-sh-er-l-s-n-i/

seisei
soon/-s-e-i-s-e-i/

seisei
now/-s-e-i-s-e-i/

sekan
knife/-s-e-k-a-n/

Sekunde
Sekondi/s-e-k-u-n-n-e/

sekyɛ
anchor/-s-e-ch-er/

sekɛɛte
skirt/-s-e-k-er-er-t-e/

selekɔn
silicon/-s-e-l-e-k-or-n/

sema

minute/-s-e-m-a/

sema
ideal/-s-e-m-a/

sempol
basic/-s-e-m-p-o-l/

semɛnte
cement/-s-e-m-er-n-t-e/

sen
pass/-s-e-n/

sen
carve/-s-e-n/

sen
more than/-s-e-n/

senamambo
thunderbolt/-s-e-n-a-m-a-m-m-o/

senamɔn
cinnamon/-s-e-n-a-m-or-n/

senasena
glossy/-s-e-n-a-s-e-n-a/

sene
cinema/-s-e-n-e/

Senegal
Senegal/s-e-n-e-g-a-l/

Senegalnyi
Senegalese/s-e-n-e-g-a-l-n-i/

Sengapɔɔ
Singapore/s-e-n-g-a-p-or-or/

Sengapɔɔnyi
Singaporean/s-e-n-g-a-p-or-or-n-i/

senke
sink/-s-e-n-k-e/

sensan
stripe/-s-e-n-s-a-n/

sera
anoint/-s-e-r-a/

sera
visit/-s-e-r-a/

sera akwan
spy/-s-e-r-a -a-q-a-n/

seraban
camp/-s-e-r-a-b-a-n/

serade
grease/-s-e-r-a-d-e/

serdaa
scarlet/-s-e-r-d-a-a/

serekye
silk/-s-e-r-e-ch-e/

serew
laugh/-s-e-r-e-w/

serew
smile/-s-e-r-e-w/

serew
funny/-s-e-r-e-w/

serɛ
thigh/-s-e-r-e-r/

serɛw
comb/-s-e-r-e-r-w/

sesaw
pick up/-s-e-s-a-w/

sese
measure/-s-e-s-e/

setiiti
street/-s-e-t-i-i-t-i/

setɔɔ

store/-s-e-t-or-or/
sew
sharpen/-s-e-w/
sɛ
if/-s-er/
sɛ
like/-s-er/
sɛ
resemble/-s-er/
sɛ
befit/-s-er/
sɛ
be fitting/-s-er/
sɛ ... a
if ... then/-s-er ... -a/
sɛbe
excuse my language/-s-er-b-e/
sɛdea
how/-s-er-d-e-a/
sɛdea-ɛte
circumstance/-s-er-d-e-a -er-t-e/
sɛe
destroy/-s-er-e/
sɛlɛri
celery/-s-e-r-l-e-r-r-i/
sɛn
hang/-s-er-n/
sɛntɔw
sentence/-s-er-n-t-or-w/
sɛso
kind/-s-er-s-o/
sɛsɛw
shrimp/-s-er-s-er-w/

si
build/-s-i/
si
happen/-s-i/
si ... do
repeat/-s-i ... -d-o/
si ... konko
auction/-s-i ... -k-o-n-k-o/
si ... nkrum
sigh/-s-i ... -n-k-r-u-m/
siane
descend/-s-i-a-n-e/
siantiri
reason/-s-i-a-n-t-i-r-i/
sider
cedi/-s-i-d-e-r/
sider
cowry/-s-i-d-e-r/
sie
bury/-s-i-e/
sie
save/-s-i-e/
siesie
tidy/-s-i-e-s-i-e/
Siɛra Leon
Sierra Leone/s-i-e-r-r-a l-e-o-n/
Siɛra Leonnyi
Sierra Leonean/s-i-e-r-r-a l-e-o-n-n-i/
sigrete
cigarette/-s-i-g-r-e-t-e/
sika
money/-s-i-k-a/

sika kɔkɔɔ
gold/-s-i-k-a -k-or-k-or-or/
sika kɔkɔɔ
gold/-s-i-k-a -k-or-k-or-or/
sin
summary/-s-i-n/
sintɔ
defect/-s-i-n-t-or/
sirete
slate/-s-i-r-e-t-e/
Siria
Syria/s-i-r-i-a/
Sirianyi
Syrian/s-i-r-i-a-n-i/
sisi
cheat/-s-i-s-i/
sisi
bear/-s-i-s-i/
sisinyi
cheater/-s-i-s-i-n-i/
sisiw
waist/-s-i-s-i-w/
siw
pound/-s-i-w/
siw
block/-s-i-w/
siw
anthill/-s-i-w/
skana
scanner/-s-k-a-n-a/
skɔlahyepe
scholarship/-s-k-or-l-a-sh-e-p-e/
Skɔtasaase

Scotland/-s-k-or-t-a-s-a-a-s-e/
skuulkɔ
schooling/-s-k-u-u-l-k-or/
skuulwienyi
graduate/-s-k-u-u-l-w-i-e-n-i/
so
reach a final milestone/-s-o/
so
be big/-s-o/
so
also/-s-o/
so dae
dream/-s-o -d-a-e/
soa
carry/-s-o-a/
sodiyɔm
sodium/-s-o-d-i-y-or-m/
soɛ
unburden/-s-o-er/
soɛe
settle/-s-o-er-e/
soɛre
arise/-s-o-e-r-r-e/
sofa
sofa/-s-o-f-a/
sofi
spade/-s-o-f-i-e/
sohori
ostrich/-s-o-h-o-r-i-e/
som
worship/-s-o-m/
som
service/-s-o-m/

soma
send/-s-o-m-a/
Somali
Somali/s-o-m-a-l-i/
Somalia
Somalia/s-o-m-a-l-i-a/
Somalianyi
Somalian/s-o-m-a-l-i-a-n-i/
sombo
value/-s-o-m-m-o/
somebo
accusation/-s-o-m-e-b-o/
somfo
waiter/-s-o-m-f-o/
son
elephant/-s-o-n/
sopa
dishonour/-s-o-p-a/
sopana
spanner/-s-o-p-a-n-a/
sordaanyi
soldier/-s-o-r-d-a-a-n-i/
sornonko
special/-s-o-r-n-o-n-k-o/
soro
above/-s-o-r-o/
soro
up/-s-o-r-o/
sorobɔnyi
angel/-s-o-r-o-b-o-r-n-i/
soroma
star/-s-o-r-o-m-a/
sosɔw

peck/-s-o-s-or-w/
sow
bear fruit/-s-o-w/
sɔ
switch on/-s-or/
sɔfo
pastor/-s-or-f-o/
sɔfopɔn
bishop/-s-or-f-o-p-or-n/
sɔlfa
sulfur/-s-or-l-f-a/
sɔn
drain/-s-or-n/
sɔnyee
collander/-s-or-n-y-e-e/
sɔpe
drop/-s-or-p-e/
sɔre
admire/-s-o-r-r-e/
sɔw
spread out/-s-or-w/
sɔw ... do
continue/-s-or-w ... -d-o/
Spen
Spain/s-p-e-n/
Spen kasa
Spanish/-s-p-e-n -k-a-s-a/
Spen kasa
Spanish/-s-p-e-n -k-a-s-a/
spese
space/-s-p-e-s-e/
sradaa
saw/-s-r-a-d-a-a/

srɛ
 beg/-s-r-e-r/
Sri Lanka
 Sri Lanka/-s-r-i l-a-n-k-a/
Sri Lankanyi
 Sri Lankan/-s-r-i l-a-n-k-a-n-i/
stediyɔm
 stadium/-s-t-e-d-i-y-or-m/
stehyɛn
 station/-s-t-e-sh-er-n/
studiyo
 studio/-s-t-u-d-i-y-o/
su
 type/-s-u/
su
 cry/-s-u/
su
 character/-s-u/
sua
 learn/-s-u-a/
sua
 study/-s-u-a/
suade
 lesson/-s-u-a-d-e/
suanyi
 learner/-s-u-a-n-i/
suapɔn
 university/-s-u-a-p-or-n/
suban
 habit/-s-u-b-a-n/
Sudan
 Sudan/-s-u-d-a-n/
Sudan Anaafo

South Sudan/-s-u-d-a-n-a-n-a-a-f-o/
Sudan Anaafonyi
 South Sudanese/-s-u-d-a-n-a-n-a-a-f-o-n-i-e/
Sudannyi
 Sudanese/-s-u-d-a-n-n-i/
suhyi
 sushi/-s-u-sh-i/
sukookoo
 lily/-s-u-k-o-o-k-o-o/
sukuu
 school/-s-u-k-u-u/
sukuudanmu
 classroom/-s-u-k-u-u-d-a-n-m-u/
sukuunyi
 student/-s-u-k-u-u-n-i-e/
sukɔnkɔn
 peacock/-s-u-k-or-n-k-or-n/
sum
 cup/-s-u-m/
suma
 hide/-s-u-m-a/
sumbui
 lead/-s-u-m-m-u-i/
sumbɔre
 tick/-s-u-m-m-o-r-r-e/
summ
 darkness/-s-u-m-m/
sundi
 pillow/-s-u-n-n-i/
sunsuando
 consequence/-s-u-n-s-u-a-n-n-o/

sunsuma
worm/-s-u-n-s-u-m-a/
sunyame
divine/-s-u-n-y-a-m-e/
supruw
island/-s-u-p-r-u-w/
suro
fear/-s-u-r-o/
suro
fear/-s-u-r-o/
susow
barb/-s-u-s-o-w/
susuw
estimate/-s-u-s-u-w/
suutu
suit/-s-u-u-t-u-o/
Swahili
Swahili/s-w-a-h-i-l-i/
Swazilande
Swaziland/s-w-az-i-l-a-n-n-e/
Swazilandenyi
Swazi/s-w-az-i-l-a-n-n-e-n-i/
t
t/-t/
ta
flatulate/-t-a/
ta
fart/-t-a/
ta
fart/-t-a/
taa
chase/-t-a-a/
taa

often/-t-a-a/
taabow
plank/-t-a-a-b-o-w/
taae
tyre/-t-a-a-e/
taahɔbɛdi
lazy/-t-a-a-h-or-b-er-d-i/
taataa
persecute/-t-a-a-t-a-a/
taban
wing/-t-a-b-a-n/
tabon
oar/-t-a-b-o-n/
tae
tie/-t-a-e/
tae-n-dae
tie-and-dye/-t-a-e-n-d-a-e/
Taeland
Thailand/t-a-e-l-a-n-n/
Taelandnyi
Thai/t-a-e-l-a-n-n-n-i/
taepe
type/-t-a-e-p-e/
taete
tithe/-t-a-e-t-e/
Taewan
Taiwan/t-a-e-w-a-n/
Taewannyi
Taiwanese/t-a-e-w-a-n-n-i/
tafere
lick/-t-a-f-e-r-e/
taferebanyimbɔmu
challenge/-t-a-f-e-r-e-b-a-n-i-m-

m-o-r-m-u/

tah
spatula/-t-a-h/

Tajekestan
Tajikstan/-t-aj-e-k-e-s-t-a-n/

Tajekestannyi
Tajik/-t-aj-e-k-e-s-t-a-n-n-i/

takontaar
turpentine/-t-a-k-o-n-t-a-a-r/

Takorade
Takoradi/t-a-k-o-r-a-d-e/

takra
feather/-t-a-k-r-a/

taksi
taxi/-t-a-k-s-i/

takua
headgear/-t-a-k-u-a/

tam
grab/-t-a-m/

tamfo
enemy/-t-a-m-f-o/

tan
hatred/-t-a-n/

tan
undesirable/-t-a-n/

tan
filthy/-t-a-n/

Tanzania
Tanzania/t-a-nz-a-n-i-a/

Tanzanianyi
Tanzanian/t-a-nz-a-n-i-a-n-i/

Tanɔ
Tano/t-a-n-or/

tare
paste/-t-a-r-e/

tawa
tobacco/-t-a-w-a/

tayaa
tile/-t-a-y-a-a/

te
hear/-t-e/

te
live/-t-e/

te
reside/-t-e/

te ... ase
understand/-t-e ... -a-s-e/

te ... nka
sense/-t-e ... -n-k-a/

te ... nka
feel/-t-e ... -n-k-a/

te apɔw
recover/-t-e -a-p-or-w/

tea
discipline/-t-e-a/

tea mu
yell/-t-e-a -m-u/

tease
living/-t-e-a-s-e/

teaseanam
chariot/-t-e-a-s-e-a-n-a-m/

tebea
location/-t-e-b-e-a/

tebɔɔ
inactive/-t-e-b-or-or/

tee

straight/-t-e-e/

teetee
harass/-t-e-e-t-e-e/

tema
empathy/-t-e-m-a/

tena
remain/-t-e-n-a/

tena
sit/-t-e-n-a/

tenabea
habitat/-t-e-n-a-b-e-a/

tene
straighten/-t-e-n-e/

tenenee
upright/-t-e-n-e-n-e-e/

tenten
long/-t-e-n-t-e-n/

tenten
tall/-t-e-n-t-e-n/

tenten
length/-t-e-n-t-e-n/

tera
cross/-t-e-r-a/

terew
slip/-t-e-r-e-w/

tesɛ
like/-t-e-s-er/

tete
antiquity/-t-e-t-e/

tete
ancient/-t-e-t-e/

tete
parent/-t-e-t-e/

tetekwaa
outdated/-t-e-t-e-q-a-a/

tetɛw
bud/-t-e-t-er-w/

tew
reduce/-t-e-w/

tew
tear/-t-e-w/

tew
pluck/-t-e-w/

tew
found/-t-e-w/

tɛ
test/-t-er/

Tɛɛki
Turkey/t-er-er-k-i/

Tɛɛkinyi
Turk/t-er-er-k-i-n-i/

Tɛkemɛnestan
Turkmenistan/-t-er-k-e-m-er-n-e-s-t-a-n/

Tɛkemɛnestannyi
Turkmen/-t-er-k-e-m-er-n-e-s-t-a-n-n-i/

tɛkyerɛma
tongue/-t-e-r-ch-e-r-e-r-m-a/

tɛlɛfoon
phone/-t-er-l-er-f-o-o-n/

tɛlɛvihyɛn
television/-t-er-l-er-v-i-sh-er-n/

tɛnɛsaene
Tennessine/-t-er-n-er-s-a-e-n-e/

tɛtrɛɛ

flat/-t-e-r-t-t-r-e-r-e-r/

tɛw
 tail/-t-er-w/

ti
 ladle/-t-i/

tia
 oppose/-t-i-a/

tia
 brief/-t-i-a/

tia
 step/-t-i-a/

tia
 minor/-t-i-a/

tiafi
 poop/-t-i-a-f-i/

tiatia
 short/-t-i-a-t-i-a/

tibowa
 conscience/-t-i-b-o-w-a/

tibɔne
 wicked/-t-i-b-or-n-e/

tidwereba
 skull/-t-i-d-w-e-r-e-b-a/

tie
 listen/-t-i-e/

tiefi
 toilet/-t-i-e-f-i/

tiefi krataa
 toilet roll/-t-i-e-f-i -k-r-a-t-a-a/

tieni
 listener/-t-i-e-n-i/

tii
 tea/-t-i-i/

tiihyɛɛte
 t-shirt/-t-i-i-sh-er-er-t-e/

tikiti
 ticket/-t-i-k-i-t-i/

tim
 stamp/-t-i-m/

timtimni
 printer/-t-i-m-t-i-m-n-i/

tinsa
 dowry/-t-i-n-s-a/

tiri
 head/-t-i-r-i/

tiri
 chapter/-t-i-r-i/

tirimuden
 wickedness/-t-i-r-i-m-u-d-e-n/

tirimumbɔbɔr
 leniency/-t-i-r-i-m-u-m-m-o-r-b-o-r-r/

tirimupɔw
 purpose/-t-i-r-i-m-u-p-o-r-w/

tiripae
 headache/-t-i-r-i-p-a-e/

tiriyi
 haircut/-t-i-r-i-y-i/

titi
 pinch/-t-i-t-i/

titiriw
 important/-t-i-t-i-r-i-w/

Tito
 Titus/-t-i-t-o/

tiw
 pursue/-t-i-w/

to
 bake/-t-o/

to
 buttocks/-t-o/

to ... monaa
 rape/-t-o ... -m-o-n-a-a/

to adi
 state/-t-o -a-d-i/

toa
 jar/-t-o-a/

Togo
 Togo/t-o-g-o/

Togonyi
 Togolese/t-o-g-o-n-i-e/

tokuro
 hole/-t-o-k-u-r-o/

tomfo
 blacksmith/-t-o-m-f-o/

toonoo
 bumblebee/-t-o-o-n-o-o/

topae
 bomb/-t-o-p-a-e/

toto
 roast/-t-o-t-o/

totorobɛnto
 trumpet/-t-o-t-o-r-o-b-e-r-n-t-o/

totɔ
 purchase/-t-o-t-or/

totɔtotɔ
 chickenpox/-t-o-t-or-t-o-t-or/

tow
 sing/-t-o-w/

tow

 throw/-t-o-w/

tow
 levy/-t-o-w/

tow
 shoot/-t-o-w/

tow ... gu
 throw away/-t-o-w ... -g-u/

tow ... kyene
 discard/-t-o-w ... -ch-e-n-e/

tow ... mu
 close/-t-o-w ... -m-u/

tow aba
 vote/-t-o-w -a-b-a/

tow abasa
 march/-t-o-w -a-b-a-s-a/

tɔ
 fall/-t-or/

tɔ
 buy/-t-or/

tɔ ... mu
 fall into/-t-or ... -m-u/

tɔ nko
 doze/-t-or -n-k-o/

tɔfe
 toffee/-t-or-f-e/

tɔmbɛr
 tumbler/-t-o-r-m-m-e-r-r/

tɔn
 sell/-t-or-n/

tɔnnyi
 seller/-t-or-n-n-i/

tɔw
 lump/-t-or-w/

trae
 try/-t-r-a-e/
trafeke
 traffic/-t-r-a-f-e-k-e/
trɛsui
 area/-t-r-e-r-s-u-i/
trɛtrɛ
 width/-t-r-e-r-t-r-e-r/
trɛw
 spread/-t-r-e-r-w/
trɔke
 truck/-t-r-o-r-k-e/
trɔma
 morsel/-t-r-o-r-m-a/
trɔsa
 trouser/-t-r-o-r-s-a/
trɔtrɔ
 van/-t-r-o-r-t-r-o-r/
ts
 ts/-t-s/
tu
 fly/-t-u/
tu
 much/-t-u/
tu ... fo
 advise/-t-u ... -f-o/
tu kwan
 travel/-t-u -q-a-n/
tu mbogya
 bleed/-t-u -m-m-o-j-a/
tu nguan
 run/-t-u -n-g-u-a-n/
tua

 pay/-t-u-a/
tuatew
 rebellion/-t-u-a-t-e-w/
tuatewnyi
 rebel/-t-u-a-t-e-w-n-i/
tuei
 pierce/-t-u-e-i/
tugu
 abortion/-t-u-g-u-o/
tumfo
 powerful/-t-u-m-f-o/
tumfuru
 glutton/-t-u-m-f-u-r-u-o/
tumfuru
 greedy/-t-u-m-f-u-r-u-o/
tumi
 be able to/-t-u-m-i-e/
tumi
 authority/-t-u-m-i-e/
tumi
 can/-t-u-m-i-e/
tumm
 dark/-t-u-m-m/
tun
 bum/-t-u-n/
Tunihyia
 Tunisia/t-u-n-i-sh-i-a/
Tunihyianyi
 Tunisian/t-u-n-i-sh-i-a-n-i/
tuntum
 black/-t-u-n-t-u-m/
tuntuma
 pillar/-t-u-n-t-u-m-a/

ture
garden/-t-u-r-e/

turu
gun/-t-u-r-u-o/

tutu
dig/-t-u-t-u-o/

tutu
early/-t-u-t-u-o/

Tuvalu
Tuvalu/t-u-v-a-l-u/

tuwiite
tweet/-t-u-w-i-i-t-e/

twa
cut/-t-w-a/

twa .. mu
cancel/-t-w-a .. -m-u/

twa ... ano
interrupt/-t-w-a ... -a-n-o/

twa ... ho hyia
surround/-t-w-a ... -h-o -sh-i-a/

twa ... mfonyin
photograph/-t-w-a ... -m-f-o-n-i-n/

twako
chalk/-t-w-a-k-o/

twann
elastic/-t-w-a-n-n/

twe
pull/-t-w-e/

twe
withdraw/-t-w-e/

twe ... aso
punish/-t-w-e ... -a-s-o/

twe ... mu
stretch/-t-w-e ... -m-u/

twe ... nyinkunu
be jealous/-t-w-e ... -n-i-n-k-u-n-u-o/

twe ... siane
download/-t-w-e ... -s-i-a-n-e/

twe breeke
brake/-t-w-e -b-r-e-e-k-e/

twe manso
litigate/-t-w-e -m-a-n-s-o/

twe mpena
date/-t-w-e -m-p-e-n-a/

tweaa
chwia/-t-w-e-a-a/

twee
mtchew/-t-w-e-e/

twere
lean on/-t-w-e-r-e/

twereduampɔn
dependable/-t-w-e-r-e-d-u-a-m-p-o-r-n/

twerɛbo
flint/-t-w-e-r-e-r-b-o/

twerɛw
scrape/-t-w-e-r-e-r-w/

tweɔn
wait/-t-w-e-or-n/

twɛ
vagina/-t-w-er/

Twi
Twi/t-w-i/

twitwa

slice/-t-w-i-t-w-a/
twitwiw
scrub/-t-w-i-t-w-i-w/
twuobuei
choboi/-t-w-u-o-b-u-e-i/
u
u/-u/
ukelele
ukelele/-u-k-e-l-e-l-e/
Ururimi
Ururimi/-u-r-u-r-i-m-i/
Uzebɛkestan
Uzbekistan/uz-e-b-er-k-e-s-t-a-n/
Uzebɛkestannyi
Uzbek/uz-e-b-er-k-e-s-t-a-n-n-i/
v
v/-v/
vaelɛt
violet/-v-a-e-l-er-t/
vakum
vacuum/-v-a-k-u-m/
vem
enthusiasm/-v-e-m/
Venizuwela
Venezuela/-v-e-n-iz-u-w-e-l-a/
Venizuwelanyi
Venezuelan/-v-e-n-iz-u-w-e-l-a-n-i/
vɛɛhyɛn
version/-v-er-er-sh-er-n/
vidio
video/-v-i-d-i-o/
Viyɛtnam

Vietnam/-v-i-y-er-t-n-a-m/
Viyɛtnamnyi
Vietnamese/-v-i-y-er-t-n-a-m-n-i/
vɔdka
vodka/-v-or-d-k-a/
vɔlum
volume/-v-or-l-u-m/
w
w/-w/
wa
be lengthy/-w-a/
waa
just/-w-a-a/
waakye
waache/-w-a-a-ch-e/
waduru
mortar/-w-a-d-u-r-u-o/
wae
peel off/-w-a-e/
wae
heh/-w-a-e/
waefae
wifi/-w-a-e-f-a-e/
wansan
deer/-w-a-n-s-a-n/
wansema
fly/-w-a-n-s-e-m-a/
wansena
housefly/-w-a-n-s-e-n-a/
wansena pobi
blowfly/-w-a-n-s-e-n-a -p-o-b-i-e/
wanta

mist/-w-a-n-t-a/

wao
wow/-w-a-o/

ware
marry/-w-a-r-e/

wate
watch/-w-a-t-e/

waw
cough/-w-a-w/

we
chew/-w-e/

we
be last/-w-e/

wea
crawl/-w-e-a/

weɛ
aye/-w-e-er/

wekɔ
fine/-w-e-k-or/

wene
bitter/-w-e-n-e/

wene
weave/-w-e-n-e/

wensee
tough/-w-e-n-s-e-e/

wentwiwentwi
squabbles/-w-e-n-t-w-i-w-e-n-t-w-i/

weɔn
guard/-w-e-or-n/

wer
canvas/-w-e-r/

were

parched/-w-e-r-e/

werɛ firi
forget/-w-e-r-e-r -f-i-r-i/

wesee
poor/-w-e-s-e-e/

weyi
this/-w-e-y-i/

wɛbsaete
website/-w-er-b-s-a-e-t-e/

wɛda
weather/-w-er-d-a/

wia
steal/-w-i-a/

wiade
world/-w-i-a-d-e/

wie
finish/-w-i-e/

wie
end/-w-i-e/

wigyinae
noon/-w-i-j-i-n-a-e/

wii
marijuana/-w-i-i/

wimu
sky/-w-i-m-u/

wimuhyɛn
aeroplane/-w-i-m-u-sh-er-n/

wimuhyɛn-gyinabea
airport/-w-i-m-u-sh-er-n-j-i-n-a-b-e-a/

wini
leak/-w-i-n-i/

winwin

whine/-w-i-n-w-i-n/

wisa
 cilantro/-w-i-s-a/

wisaba
 coriander/-w-i-s-a-b-a/

wo
 your/-w-o/

wo
 you/-w-o/

wo tiri nkwa o
 happy birthday/-w-o -t-i-r-i -n-q-a -o/

woana
 who/-w-o-a-n-a/

woana ne
 whose/-w-o-a-n-a -n-e/

woanasodi
 accountability/-w-o-a-n-a-s-o-d-i-e/

woho
 yourself/-w-o-h-o/

wole
 cowhide/-w-o-l-e/

woo
 birth/-w-o-o/

worɔw
 strip off/-w-o-r-o-r-w/

wosaw
 masticate/-w-o-s-a-w/

wosee
 dry/-w-o-s-e-e/

wosow
 quake/-w-o-s-o-w/

wɔ
 one/-w-or/

wɔ
 stab/-w-or/

wɔ
 be/-w-or/

wɔ
 have/-w-or/

wɔ
 at/-w-or/

wɔ
 they/-w-or/

wɔ ... mu
 inside/-w-or ... -m-u/

wɔ ... pande
 inject/-w-or ... -p-a-n-n-e/

wɔdin
 famous/-w-or-d-i-n/

wɔfa
 uncle/-w-or-f-a/

wɔfase
 nephew/-w-or-f-a-s-e/

wɔfasewa
 niece/-w-or-f-a-s-e-w-a/

Wɔlɔf
 Wolof/w-or-l-or-f/

wɔmba
 pestle/-w-or-m-m-a/

wɔnde
 theirs/-w-or-n-n-e/

wɔw
 prop/-w-or-w/

wu

die/-w-u/
wudinyi
murderer/-w-u-d-i-n-i/
wui
dead/-w-u-i/
Wukuda
Wednesday/w-u-k-u-d-a/
wunyane
resurrection/-w-u-n-y-a-n-e/
wura
master/-w-u-r-a/
wura
owner/-w-u-r-a/
wuramu
bush/-w-u-r-a-m-u/
wusa
alligator pepper/-w-u-s-a/
wusiw
smoke/-w-u-s-i-w/
y
y/-y/
ya
wild/-y-a/
Yaa
Yaa/y-a-a/
yafunu
belly/-y-a-f-u-n-u-o/
Yakobo
James/y-a-k-o-b-o/
yamu
abdomen/-y-a-m-u/
yamukaw
stomach-ache/-y-a-m-u-k-a-w/

yantamm
wide/-y-a-n-t-a-m-m/
yare
be ill/-y-a-r-e/
yare
disease/-y-a-r-e/
yareba
sickness/-y-a-r-e-b-a/
yaredɔm
plague/-y-a-r-e-d-o-r-m/
yarenyi
patient/-y-a-r-e-n-i/
yaresa
healing/-y-a-r-e-s-a/
yaw
painful/-y-a-w/
yaw
pain/-y-a-w/
Yaw
Yaw/y-a-w/
Yawda
Thursday/y-a-w-d-a/
Yehowa
Jehovah/y-e-h-o-w-a/
yem
impregnate/-y-e-m/
yera
disappear/-y-e-r-a/
yere
wife/-y-e-r-e/
yere
hassle/-y-e-r-e/
yerɛyerɛw

acidic/-y-e-r-e-r-y-e-r-e-r-w/

Yesu
 Jesus/y-e-s-u/

yew
 get lost/-y-e-w/

yɛ
 be/-y-er/

yɛ
 we/-y-er/

yɛ
 make/-y-er/

yɛ
 do/-y-er/

yɛ … aduru
 bewitch/-y-e-r … -a-d-u-r-u-o/

yɛ … asotie
 obey/-y-er … -a-s-o-t-i-e/

yɛ … atuu
 embrace/-y-er … -a-t-u-u/

yɛ … ayeforo
 wed/-y-e-r … -a-y-e-f-o-r-o/

yɛ … wie
 achieve/-y-er … -w-i-e/

yɛ … yie
 fix/-y-er … -y-i-e/

yɛ adwuma
 work/-y-er -a-d-w-u-m-a/

yɛ akaw
 cut ties/-y-er -a-k-a-w/

yɛ biribi
 act/-y-e-r -b-i-r-i-b-i/

yɛ dwei
 be emotionally charged/-y-er

-d-w-e-i/

yɛ fɛw
 be beautiful/-y-er -f-er-w/

yɛayie
 good job/-y-er-a-y-i-e/

yɛbea
 manner/-y-er-b-e-a/

yɛhubida
 familiar/-y-er-h-u-b-i-d-a/

Yɛmɛn
 Yemen/y-er-m-er-n/

Yɛmɛnnyi
 Yemeni/y-er-m-er-n-n-i/

yɛnnhubida
 unfamiliar/-y-er-n-n-h-u-b-i-d-a/

yi
 remove/-y-i/

yi
 these/-y-i/

yi
 select/-y-i/

yi … adi
 reveal/-y-i … -a-d-i/

yi … adi
 fire/-y-i … -a-d-i/

yi … ani
 look away/-y-i … -a-n-i/

yi … ano
 answer/-y-i … -a-n-o/

yi … asotiw
 alert/-y-i … -a-s-o-t-i-w/

yi … ayɛw
 praise/-y-i … -a-y-er-w/

yi ... do
deduct/-y-i ... -d-o/

yi ... ma
betray/-y-i ... -m-a/

yi ... so
subtract/-y-i ... -s-o/

yi mpataa
fish/-y-i -m-p-a-t-a-a/

yi tow
donate/-y-i -t-o-w/

yi yɛ kwasea ae
foolish/-y-i -y-er -q-a-s-e-a -a-e/

yie
well/-y-i-e/

yie
be good/-y-i-e/

yie
better/-y-i-e/

yiedi
prosperity/-y-i-e-d-i/

yieyɛ
goodness/-y-i-e-y-er/

yikyerɛ
revelation/-y-i-ch-e-r-e-r/

yikyerɛ
film/-y-i-ch-e-r-e-r/

yindam
razor/-y-i-n-n-a-m/

yinom
these/-y-i-n-o-m/

yiri
overflow/-y-i-r-i/

yiye

efficiency/-y-i-y-e/

yiyeyɛ
wellbeing/-y-i-y-e-y-er/

Yohanes
John/y-o-h-a-n-e-s/

yomo
dye/-y-o-m-o/

yoo
okay/-y-o-o/

Yoruba
Yoruba/y-o-r-u-b-a/

Yuganda
Uganda/y-u-g-a-n-n-a/

Yugandanyi
Ugandan/y-u-g-a-n-n-a-n-i/

Yukren
Ukraine/y-u-k-r-e-n/

Yukrennyi
Ukrainean/y-u-k-r-e-n-n-i/

yunete
unit/-y-u-n-e-t-e/

Yurop
Europe/y-u-r-o-p/

yuso
use/-y-u-s-o/

Zambia
Zambia/z-a-m-m-i-a/

zambiani
Zambian/z-a-m-m-i-a-n-i/

Zembabuwe
Zimbabwe/z-e-m-m-a-b-u-w-e/

Zembabuwenyi
Zimbabwean/z-e-m-m-a-b-u-w-

e-n-i/
zep
  zip/*z-e-p*/
zu
  zoo/*z-u*/

English - Asante Twi

Entries in the English - Asante Twi section are arranged in this order:

'a b c d e f g h i j k l m n o p q r s t u v w x y z

a
ngyetomu
access
a
hokwan
a
accident
a bit
akwanhyia
kakraabi
account
a little
kontaa
kakra
accountability
abdomen
woanasodi
yamu
accounts
Abena
nkontaa
Abena
Accra
able
Nkran
seadeyɛ
accusation
abochi
somebɔ
abokyi
accuse
abomination
bɔ ... somebɔ
akyiwade
achieve
aborigine
yɛ ... wie
abɔasee
achievement
abortion
mmɔdemmɔ
tugu
acidic
about
yerɛyerɛw
fa ... ho
act
above
agofa
soro
act
abroad
yɛ biribi
aburokyire
action
abundant
nyɛe
abuwdo
active
accept
hyewhyew
gye ... to mu
activity
acceptance
dwuma

ad
guamudawurbɔ

adapt
dane

add
fa ... ka ho

addition
ntodo

address
adrɛse

ademe
ademe

adjective
dintamsi

adjust
fekyere

administration
kuwbu

admire
sɔre

adopt
gye ... yɛn

adoption
abanɛn

adulation
ayɛyi

adult
panin

adultery
ayerfa

advance
adɔntene

advantage

dwudwu

adverb
nyɛetamsi

advertise
bɔ ... ho dawuru

advice
afotu

advise
tu ... fo

advocate
dimafo

aeroplane
wimuhyɛn

Afghan
Afganestanni

Afghanistan
Afganestan

Africa
Abibir

African
bibir

African
abibir

African Union
Abibiman Nkabomkuw

Afrikaans
Afrikanse

afternoon
awiabere

again
biom

age
nin

age
nimfe
age group
mfɛfo
aggression
akokɔbirisɛm
agree
pene
ah
aa
aid
mmoa
aim
botae
airport
wimuhyɛn-gyinabea
Ajoa
Adwoa
Akan
Akan
Akuapem
Akuapem
alcohol
nsah
alert
yi ... asotiw
Algeria
Ɔlgyeria
algorithm
algoredeme
alhaji
alaagyi
all

nina
all
ninara
allergic
alɛgyiki
allergy
alɛgyi
alligator
mampam
alligator pepper
wusa
allow
ma ... kwan
almighty
ɔdomankoma
Almighty
Nyankopɔn
alone
nko
alphabet
akyerɛwamma
also
so
aluminium
aluminiyɔm
always
aberebiara
am
yɛ
Ama
Amma
amazing
nwanwa

ambassador
 booni
amen
 amen
America
 Amɛreka
American
 Amɛrekani
Amharic
 Amarinya
among
 ntamu
ampay
 ampe
ancestor
 nana
anchor
 sekyɛ
ancient
 tete
ancient times
 nkaano
and
 na
angel
 sorobɔni
anger
 abufuw
angle
 kwanɛn
Angola
 Angola
Angolan

 Angolani
animal
 abowa
ankle
 nannwɛ
announce
 fa ... to gua
announcement
 amanneɛbɔ
annoy
 gyegye
annoyance
 ahisɛm
annoying
 ahi
annul
 gu
anoint
 sera
another
 koroso
answer
 yi ... ano
answer
 mmuae
ant
 pataakowa
Antartica
 Antaateka
antelope
 ɔtwe
anthill
 siw

antiquity
tete
ants
nkran
anvil
atommo
any
biara
apathy
akwadwere
ape
adɔpe
apparition
kakae
appellation
nsabran
apple
aper
application
aplekehyɛn
appreciate
ani sɔ
approach
bɛn
apricot
eprikɔt
April
Ebɔbira
Arctic
Aktek
are
yɛ
area

trɛsui
area
brɔn
argon
aagɔn
argue
di ... kyim
argument
kyim
arise
soɛre
arm
abasa
Armenia
Aminia
Armenian
Aminiani
armpit
ammaade
around
ho
arrange
hyehyɛ
arrive
du
arrogant
dwɛɛ
arrow
bɛn
artery
akomantini
as
mmrɛ

ash
nso

Asia
Ahyia

ask
bisa

ask ... out
se ... pɛ

aspiration
daekɛse

assessment
nsɔhwɛ

asset
ahonyade

assistant
boafo

association
fɛkuw

at
wɔ

athlete
atliti

Atlantic
Atlantek

atom
atɔm

attach
fam

attire
afade

auction
si ... konko

August
Difuu

aunt
ante

Australia
Ɔstreliya

author
kyerɛwni

authoritative
kasaprɛko

authority
tumi

autism
ɔtisim

Autumn
Powbere

avoid
kwatiri

aw
ɔ

awaken
nyane

award
abasobɔde

awesome
ahunabɔbirim

axe
abɔnnua

ay
e

aye
weɛ

ayoyo
ayoyo

Azerbaijan
Azɛbaegyan
Azerbaijani
Azɛbaegyanni
azonto
azonto
b
b
baboon
akɔnsɔn
baby
abofra
back
akyiri
back of the head
atikɔ
backyard
fikyiri
bad
bɔne
badge
abɔbaado
bag
baage
Bahrain
Baren
Bahraini
Barenni
bake
to
ball
bɔɔl
balloon

balun
banana
kwadu
Bangladesh
Bangladɛhye
Bangladeshi
Bangladɛhyeni
bank
banke
banku
banku
baptise
bɔ ... asu
baptism
anuma
barb
susow
bargain
di ... ano
bark
puow
bark
abon
barrel
ankora
barren
bɔnin
basic
sempol
basin
bɛɛsen
basket
kentɛn

basketball
 kɛntɛn-bɔɔlbɔ
bat
 pan
bathe
 guare
bathroom
 aguaree
battery
 batri
battle
 di ... sa
battle
 sa
be
 yɛ
be
 wɔ
be able to
 tumi
be beautiful
 yɛ fɛw
be big
 so
be cooked
 bene
be defeated
 di nkogu
be drunk
 bow
be emotionally charged
 yɛ dwei
be evil

 muo
be fitting
 sɛ
be good
 yie
be guilty of
 di ... fɔ
be high
 krɔn
be ill
 yare
be jealous
 twe ... ninkunu
be last
 we
be lengthy
 wa
be pregnant
 ninsɛn
be relevant to
 fa ... ho
be satisfied
 mee
be shy
 fɛre
be trivial
 da famu
be wrong
 bowa
beach
 mpoano
bead
 ahonne

beaker
 pentoa
bean
 aduwa
bear
 sisi
bear fruit
 sow
beard
 abɔdwesɛ
beat
 boro
beautiful
 fɛw
beauty
 ahoɔfɛw
because
 ɛfirisɛ
become
 hyɛ ase yɛ
become famous
 gye din
bed
 mpa
bedbug
 mpurkaa
bedroom
 pia
bedstead
 mpadua
bee
 adowa
beef

 nantwinam
beer
 biɛɛ
beetle
 abebɛ
befit
 sɛ
before
 ana
befriend
 fa ... adamfo
beg
 srɛ
begin
 hyɛ ... ase
beginning
 ahyɛase
behaviour
 braban
behind
 akyi
behind
 awiei
being
 nimpa
belch
 puw
believe
 gye ... di
bell
 adɔmma
belly
 yafunu

belly button
 mfuruma
beloved
 dɔfo
belt
 abɔdo
bench
 bɛnkye
bend
 koa
Benin
 Bɛnin
Beninois
 Bɛninni
beryllium
 beriliyɔm
best
 kamakamakama
betray
 yi ... ma
better
 yie
bewitch
 yɛ ... aduru
Bhutan
 Butan
Bhutann
 Butanni
bible
 baebol
bicycle
 baesekel
big

 kɛse
bile
 bɔwen
billhook
 adare
billion
 ɔpepem-apem
billy
 nin
biology
 bayolɔgyi
bird
 anoma
birth
 woo
birth
 awoo
birthday
 awoda
bishop
 sɔfopɔn
Bissau-Guinean
 Bisaw-Ginini
bite
 ka
bitter
 wene
black
 tuntum
blacksmith
 tomfo
blanket
 kuntu

blazing
huoo

bleach
pɔre

bleed
tu mmogya

bleeding
mmogyatu

bless
hyira

blessing
nhyira

blindness
anifura

block
siw

blog
blɔge

blood
mmogya

blow
huw

blow
kutuku

blowfly
wansena pobi

blue
bruu

boat
ɔkorow

bodice
bɔdes

body

honamdua

boil
huru

boil
pɔmpɔ

boiled herbs
dudo

bomb
topae

bone
biew

bonus
ntoso

book
buukuu

borehole
burabɔn

boron
borɔn

borrow
firi

boss
adwumapanin

both
anu

bother
haw

bother
haw

Botswana
Bɔtswana

bottle
bɔdammɔ

bow
 agyan
bow-legged
 ananta
bowl
 ayowa
box
 adaka
boxing
 kutukubɔ
boy
 banimma
boyfriend
 mpena
braid
 dwow
brain
 ahuon
brake
 twe breeke
brake
 breeke
branch
 mane
branch
 korbata
brave
 katakyi
Brazzaville-Congolese
 Brazavel-Kongoni
bread
 abodoo
break

bu
breakfast
 anapaduan
breast
 numfo
breastmilk
 numfonsu
breath
 ahome
breathe
 gu ahome
bribe
 mmoaba
bribery
 kɛtɛasehyɛ
brick
 brekese
bride
 ayeforo
bridegroom
 ayeforokunu
bridge
 bregye
brief
 tia
bright
 kann
bring
 de ... ba
brook
 ɔkye
broom
 mena

broomstick
menaba
brother
nua-banin
brown
ntokowantokowa
bruise
birim
Brunei
Brunae
Bruneian
Brunaeni
brush
borɔsow
bucket
bokiti
bud
tetɛw
bud
kukuduuduw
budget
bɔgyɛte
buffalo
bufalo
build
si
building
dan
bullet
korabo
bully
patapaani
bully

bɔ ... patapaa
bullying
patapaa
bum
tun
bumblebee
toonoo
bump into
pem
bungalow
fitia
burden
adesoa
burglary
krɔnoo
burgle
bɔ ... krɔnoo
Burkina Faso
Bɔkina Faso
Burkinabe
Bɔkina Fasoni
burn
hyehye
Burundi
Burunni
Burundian
Burunnini
bury
sie
bus
bɔs
bus conductor
metini

bush
 wuramu
business
 guadi
but
 naaso
butcher
 bɔnamni
butter
 bɔta
butterfly
 fafranta
buttocks
 to
button
 baten
buy
 tɔ
buyer
 pɛni
by
 ho
by any chance
 agyɛngyɛmmiara
bye
 nkra
cabbage
 fan
cake
 aboloo
calabash
 krowa
calcium
 kalsiyɔm
calculus
 mmobasante twi
calendar
 kalɛnna
calf
 nantu
call
 frɛ
calm
 dwedwe
Cambodia
 Kammodia
Cambodian
 Kammodiani
came
 baee
camel
 efupɔnkɔ
camera
 kamera
Cameroon
 Kamerun
camp
 seraban
campaign
 kampen
can
 tumi
Canada
 Kanada
cancel
 twa .. mu

cancer
 kokoram
cane
 abae
cannon
 prɛm
canoe
 hɛmma
canvas
 wer
capable
 kwabran
capital
 ahenekurow
capsid
 akate
captain
 kyapem
car
 kaar
carbon
 kaabɔn
card
 kaade
care
 hwɛ ... yie
careful
 hwɛyiehwɛyie
carefully
 ahwɛyiemu
carefulness
 ahwɛyie
caress

fefa
Caribbean
 Karibiyɛn
carpenter
 kapentani
carpentry
 kapentadwuma
carpet
 kapɛt
carrot
 karɔte
carry
 soa
carton
 kaaton
cartoon
 kaatun
carve
 sen
cash
 dwɛɛtɛɛ
cassava
 bankye
cast
 agofomma
castanet
 firikyiwa
castle
 abannan
cat
 agyinammowa
catarrh
 atibɛn

catch
 kye
catechumen
 kristoni foforo
category
 kyɛkuw
caterpillar
 ntuntu
cause itchiness
 keka
cease
 gyae
cedi
 sider
celery
 sɛlɛri
cement
 semɛnte
centipede
 sakasaka
Central African
 Abibir Finimfin Manni
Central African Republic
 Abibir Finimfin Man
centre
 finimfin
century
 mfeha
certificate
 abɔdinkrataa
ch
 ky
Chad

Kyead
Chadian
 Kyeadni
chain
 pokyere
chair
 agua
chairperson
 guamutenani
chalk
 twako
challenge
 taferebanimmɔmu
chameleon
 abosomanketew
chamomile
 kamomael
champion
 katakyi
change
 nsesa
chaotic
 manamana
chapter
 tiri
character
 su
charcoal
 biriw
charge
 kyeagye
chariot
 teaseanam

chase
taa
cheap
fo
cheat
sisi
cheater
sisini
cheek
afono
cheese
kyiis
cheetah
kyiita
chef
hyɛfe
chemistry
kɛmistiri
cheque
kyɛke
chest
akoko
chew
we
chicken
akokɔ
chickenpox
totɔtotɔ
chief
hene
child
ba
childbirth

abawoo
childhood
mmafoberemu
children
mma
chimpanzee
kontoromfi
chin
abɔdwe
China
Kyeaena
Chinese
Kyeaenani
chisel
pɛe
chives
anwewba
chlorine
klorin
choboi
twuobuei
chocolate
kyeɔkɔlete
Christ
Kristo
Christian
kristoni
Christianity
kristosom
Christmas
Bronya
church
asɔre

chwia
 tweaa
cigarette
 sigrete
cilantro
 wisa
cinema
 sene
cinnamon
 senamɔn
circle
 kanko
circumstance
 sɛdea -ɛte
citizen
 mamma
city
 kurowkɛse
civil war
 amanko
civilized
 hyehyɛpɛ
clap
 bɔ nsamu
clarion
 dedepefee
class
 mangow
classroom
 sukuudanmu
clay
 dɛte
clean

 kita ... ho
clear
 pen
clearly
 pefee
clever
 aniwaseatew
click
 kleke
climb
 fow
clinic
 ayaresabea
clock
 dɔnkyerɛ
close
 tow ... mu
cloth
 ntama
clothes
 ntare
cloud
 muna
cloud
 mununkum
cloudy
 musumunsum
clove
 hwenteaba
coach
 kookyi
coaltar
 kootaa

coast
mpoano
coat
kootu
cobra
kyemmiri
cockerel
akokɔnin
cockroach
kakarika
cocoa
kokoo
coconut
kube
cocoyam
mankani
cocoyam leaves
kontommire
code
koodu
coffee
kɔfe
coin
kɔen
cold
nwin
collander
sɔnyee
collect
gye
college
kolegyi
color

ahosu
colour
kala
comb
serɛw
comb
afe
come
ba
come
bra
comfort
ahomeka
coming
mmae
comma
kɔma
command
hyɛ
command
nhyɛ
commend
kamfo
committee
kɔnomtii
community
akuraa
Comoran
Kɔmɔrɔsni
company
adwumakuw
compassion
ayamuhyehye

compensation
 akatua
competition
 asante twisi
computer
 kɔmpiyuta
computing
 nkontaabu
concubine
 mpena
condolences
 due
conference
 ahyiadi
confidence
 awerɛhyɛmu
confusion
 bisibisibasaa
congenial
 hyiahiano
Congo
 Kongo
Congo-Brazzaville
 Brazavel-Kongo
Congo-Kinshasa
 Kinhyɛasa-Kongo
congratulations
 mmo
conjunctivitis
 apolo
conqueror
 bɔaman
conscience

 tibowa
consequence
 sunsuanno
consolation
 awerɛkyekyer
constituency
 abatowmpɔtam
construct
 dwin
contempt
 animtia
content
 de a ɛwɔ mu
continent
 asaasetaw
continue
 sɔw ... do
control
 di ... so
controversy
 ntawantawa
converse
 di nkɔmmɔ
cook
 noa
cool
 dwe
cool
 dwee
coop
 buw
cooperation
 nnɔboa

cooperative
nnoboa
copper
kupa
coriander
wisaba
corn
aburow
corner
kokoa
corners
afanaa
corpse
funu
corruption
prɔwyɛ
cost
kaw
Cote d'Ivoire
Asommɛn Mpoano
cottage
dan kete
cotton
adigidɔn
couch
kawokye
cough
bɔ waw
cough
waw
could
tumiee
councillor

baguani
count
kan
country
man
courage
akokoduru
courier
bɔfo
court
asɛnniibea
courtship
mpenatwe
cousin
nua
covenant
apam
cover
fura
covetuousness
anibere
cow
nantwi
cowhide
wole
cowry
sider
crab
kɔtɔ
crawl
wea
create
bɔ

creation
abɔde

creator
bɔade

cripple
bubuani

crocodile
dɛnkyɛm

cross
tera

cross
mmeamudua

crow
bɔn

crow
akonkoran

crowd
dɔm

crown
ahenekyɛw

crumble
dwiriw

cry
su

cryptolepis sanguinolenta
nibima

crystal
hyɛnhyɛmmo

cube
kuubu

cubit
bafa

culture
amammere

cumin
kamin

cunning
nyansanansa

cup
kɔɔpow

cup
sum

curse
bɔ ... dua

curse
mpaa

curtain
kɛɛten

custom
amanne

customer
batani

cut
twa

cut ties
yɛ akaw

cutlass
adar

cymbal
akasa

Cypriot
Saeprɔsni

Cyprus
Saeprɔs

d
d

dad
agya
daily
daa
dam
nsuban
damsel
basiaba
dance
saw
dancing
asaw
danger
pirahu
dangerous
pirade
dark
tumm
darkness
summ
darling
dɔfo
date
afeda
date
twe mpena
daughter
babasia
dawn
ahanamakye
day
da
daybreak

adekyee
dead
wui
dear
ɔdɔ
death
owu
debate
kasabisa
debt
kaw
decade
mfedu
decagon
kwanɛn-du
deceive
daadaa
December
Mumu
deception
kohwi
decision
gyinae
deduct
yi ... do
deep
amudɔ
deer
wansan
defeat
nkogu
defecate
nye

defect
sintɔ
defile
fi gu ... ho
definition
nkyerɛkyerɛmu
deflate
dwe
delay
kyɛr
delightful
kama
deliver
mona
delivery
amonade
demand
ahiade
democracy
obiara-amammu
deny
kame
depart
fi
dependable
twereduampɔn
deplete
sa
depth
mudɔ
descend
siane
desert

sare
deserve
fata
desirable
akɔnnɔ
desire
kɔnnɔ
desire
apɛde
destiny
nkrabea
destroy
sɛe
determination
aniwaden
development
mpontu
devil
abonsam
dew
bɔw
dewdrop
bɔsu
diamond
dɛnkyɛmmo
diarrhoea
akokɔre
dice
amma
dictionary
kasasua
did
yɛee

die
wu
different
ahodow
difficult
dene
dig
tutu
dignify
di ... ni
dignity
anidifata
dimwit
bɛlɛ
dine
didi
Dinka
Dinka
dinosaur
daenoketew
dirt
fih
dirty
fih
disappear
yera
disappoint
daadaa
disappointment
nnaadaa
discard
tow ... kyene
disciple

osuani
discipline
tea
discord
ntoto
disease
yare
disgrace
gu ... anim ase
disgrace
animguase
disgusting
nkɔn
dish
prɛte
dishevelled
sakasaka
dishonour
sopa
disposition
bɔbew
dispute
gye ... akyingye
diss
hyehyɛ ... ahoroba
diss
ahorobahyehyɛ
distinguished
abrɔba
distinguished
aborɔba
distress
ahometew

distressed
basaa
district
mansin
ditch
bɔnka
diverse
aforafora
diversity
aforaforadɔm
divide
kyɛ ... mu
divine
sunyame
division
nkyekyɛmu
divorce
awaregu
Djibouti
Gyibuti
Djiboutian
Gyibutini
do
yɛ
doctor
dɔketa
doctor
fekyew
dog
kraman
doll
aboduaba
dollar

dɔla
donate
yi tow
done
ayɛ
donkey
asoaso
door
abow
doubt
akyingye
dough
mmɔre
dove
aborɔnoma
down
ase
download
twe ... siane
downstairs
asenade
dowry
tinsa
doze
tɔ nko
drain
sɔn
drama
drama
drank
nomee
draughts
dame

draw
drɔw
drawers
drɔɔse
dream
so dae
dream
dae
dress
atare
drink
nom
drive
ka
driver
hɛnkani
drop
sɔpe
drop
gyae ... to famu
drown
memem
drowsiness
anikom
drug
aduru
drum
kyene
drummer
kyerɛma
drunkard
kɔnomnsani
drunkenness

nsabow
dry
wosee
dry
hata
dry season
Ɔpɛ
duck
dabodabo
dump
bɔɔla
dumpling
bofrot
dung
bin
duration
hwere
durbar
aguabɔ
dust
mfutuw
dustpan
asawwura
Dutch
Ɔdɔkye
duty
as de
dwarf
abowatia
dye
yomo
dysmenorrhoea
brayaw

e
  ɛ

each
  biara

each and everyone
  obibiara

eagle
  ɔkɔre

ear
  asowa

early
  ntɛm

early
  tutu

earpiece
  asomuade

earring
  asowamuade

earth
  asaase

earthquake
  asaasewosow

east
  boka

East Timor
  Boka Timɔ

East Timorese
  Boka Timɔni

easy
  koko

eat
  di

eaten
  adi

ebola
  ibola

ebony
  duabo

economy
  ɛkɔnɔmi

eczema
  ɛkrɔ

education
  nwomasua

ee
  i

eel
  bereku

efficiency
  yiye

effort
  mmɔden

Efua
  Afua

egg
  kosua

eggplant
  ntropo

Egypt
  Misrim

Egyptian
  Misrimni

Eid
  Id

eight
  awɔtwe

eight days
 nnaawɔtwe
eight persons
 baawɔtwe
eighteen
 du-awɔtwe
eighty
 aduawɔtwe
Ekua
 Akua
elastic
 twann
elbow
 batwɛre
elder
 panin
election
 abatow
electric
 aninamde
electricity
 aninam
electron
 ilɛktrɔn
elephant
 son
eleven
 du-koro
email
 imel
embrace
 yɛ ... atuu
empathy

 tema
emphasis
 o
empty
 hunu
encourage
 hyɛ ... nkuran
encouragement
 nkuranhyɛ
end
 awiei
end
 wie
enema
 sa
enemy
 tamfo
energy
 adwumatumi
engine
 ingyin
engineer
 dwinni
England
 Ngyiresi
English
 borɔfo
enmity
 anitan
enter
 dua
entertain
 gye ... ani

entertaining
anika
enthusiasm
vem
entire
ninaa
entry
nnuamu
envy
ahoɔyaa
Equatorial Guinea
Malabo-Gini
Eritrea
Ɛritrea
Eritrean
Ɛritreani
err
fom
Esi
Asi
espionage
kwansera
estimate
susuw
eternal
a-ɔ-nni-awiei
eternity
mmeresanten
Ethiopia
Abesinia
Ethiopian
Abesiniani
Europe

Yurop
evening
awimmere
event
dwumadi
every
biara
everyone
obiara
everything
biribiara
everywhere
beabiara
evil
bɔne
evildoer
adebɔneyɛni
exam
nsɔhwɛ
example
mfatoho
excellence
adeaoye
excellent
buwei
except
gye
except that
mmom
exchange
fa ... sesa
excuse me
kafra

excuse my language
sɛbe

executioner
ɔbrafo

exit
puei

expensive
na

experience
ɛspiriɛns

expertise
adwinsa

explain
kyerɛ ... ase

explanation
nkyerɛase

explode
kabum

exploration
akwantu

extend
bae

extension
mmaemu

extinguish
dum

exult
di ahurusi

exultation
ntonton

eye
ani

eyeball
anikosua

eyebrow
anintɔn

eyelash
anisoatɛw

f
f

fable
kodi

fabric
ntoma

face
animu

fade
hoa

faith
gyedi

fall
tɔ

fall down
hwe ase

fall into
tɔ ... mu

falsification
dabraba

familiar
yɛhubida

family
busua

famous
wɔdin

fan
papaah

Fanti
 Fante
fare well
 baebae
farm
 kua
farmer
 kuani
fart
 ta
fart
 ta
fast
 di mmuada
fast
 hyee
fast
 ntɛm
fasting
 mmuada
fat
 bɔdɛe
fatigue
 bahaw
favor
 animpa
favouritism
 niyimu
fear
 suro
fear
 suro
feather

 takra
February
 Kwakwar
feel
 te ... nka
feeling
 atenka
fees
 fiise
feet
 nansa
fell
 tɔee
female
 basia
female
 bea
fence
 ban
fertile
 bere
festival
 afahyɛ
fetish
 bosom
fever
 atiridii
field
 agoprama
fifteen
 du-anum
fifty
 aduonum

fight
ko

figure
kaasɛ

figure of speech
kasammireni

file
faele

Filipino
Felepinsni

fill
hyɛ ... ma

fill up
hyɛ ... ma

film
yikyerɛ

filthy
tan

find
hu

fine
wekɔ

finger
nsatea

fingernail
nsa-awerɛwba

fingertip
nsaano

finish
wie

fire
gya

fire
yi ... adi

firewood
nyena

firmly
pintinn

first
a-ɛ-di-kan

first
kane

firstborn
abasante twi

fish
yi mpataa

fish
nsunam

fish-hook
nkwaba

fisherman
fareni

fishing-net
eboa

fist
kutuku

five
anum

five persons
baanum

fix
yɛ ... yie

fixer
ɔyɛadeyie

flag
frankaa

flat
  tɛtrɛɛ
flatulate
  ta
flee
  guane
flesh
  honam
flexible
  mmerɛ
flicker
  dumsɔ
flint
  twerɛbo
flood
  nsuyiri
floor
  famu
flour
  asiam
flow
  pem
flower
  nhyiren
fluorine
  flɔriin
flute
  atɛntɛbɛn
fly
  tu
fly
  wansema
fog

bɔw
fold
  bobɔw
foliage
  mfuw
follow
  di ... akyiri
folly
  nkwaseasɛm
food
  adiban
fool
  kwasea
foolish
  yi yɛ kwasea ae
foolishness
  kwaseade
foot
  nansa
football
  bɔɔlbɔ
footstep
  namɔn
for
  ma ...
forbid
  bara
force
  hyɛ
force
  animpi
forehead
  moma

foreigner
buroni

foresee
hu ... ansa

forest
kwae

forever
daadaa

forget
werɛ firi

forgetfulness
awerɛfiri

forgive
fa ... kyɛ

forgiveness
bɔnefakyɛ

fork
fɔɔke

fortress
abannennen

forty
aduanan

found
tew

foundation
fapem

four
anan

four persons
fo anan

fourteen
du-anan

fox
ɔsɔ

fraction
kyɛmu

fragrance
huam

fragrant
huahuam

framework
apa

France
Frans

frankly
penpen

free
gyaye

free
kwa

freedom
fawohodi

freezing
awɔw

French
Frɛnkyeni

French
frɛnkye

fresh
mono

friction
akasakasa

Friday
Fida

fridge
fregye

fried-fish
 kyenam
friend
 adamfo
friendly
 ayɛnkoyɛnko
friendship
 anɛnkoyɛ
frighten
 huna
frightening
 huhuuhu
frog
 atwɛre
from
 fi
frond
 mmɛnsuon
front
 animu
fruit
 aduaba
fry
 kyew
fufu
 fufu
Fula
 Fula
full
 ma
funeral
 ayi
funny

 serew
future
 daakye
g
 g
Gabon
 Gabɔn
Gabonese
 Gabɔnni
GaDangme
 Nkrankasa
gain
 nya
gall
 bɔnwoma
gallon
 galɔn
Gambia
 Gammia
Gambian
 Gammiani
game
 agoro
gang
 kuw
gap
 ɛgyerɛ
garage
 garagye
garden
 ture
garden egg
 ntrɔba

gari
gari

garlic
gaaleke

garment
ataade

gas
gaas

gaseous
gaas

gate
geeti

gather
boaboa

gaudy
kɔsɔɔ

gave
maee

Gaza
Gaza

Gazan
Gazani

Gbe
Gbe

gecko
abosomaketew

genealogy
busuasanten

generation
mmasanten

generosity
ayamuyie

genius
anɛn

gentle
dzɛn

gentleman
krakye

gently
dzɛnnzɛn

Georgia
Gyeɔgyea

Georgian
Gyeɔgyeani

German
Dɔyekye

Germany
Gyɛmɛni

germinate
fifiri

get
gye

get lost
yew

get wet
fɔw

Ghana
Gaana

Ghanaian
Gaanani

ghost
saman

giant
kraban

giant
amamfi

gift
 akyɛde
ginger
 kakaduru
ginseng
 gyensɛn
giraffe
 gyirafe
girl
 basiaba
give
 ma
glass
 gyerasee
glory
 animunyam
glossy
 senasena
glutton
 tumfuru
go
 kɔ
go mad
 bɔ dam
go to the toilet
 kɔ tiefi
goal
 gol
goat
 abirekyi
god
 nyame
godspeed

 nanteyie
gold
 sika kɔkɔɔ
gold
 sika kɔkɔɔ
gong gong
 dawuro
good
 papa
good
 pa
good afternoon
 me ma wo aha
good evening
 me ma wo adwe
good job
 yɛayie
good morning
 me ma wo akye
goodness
 yieyɛ
goosebumps
 awɔse
gospel
 asɛmpa
gossip
 di ... kɔnkɔnsa
gossip
 anokum
got
 gyeee
govern
 bu ... man

governance
amammu

government
aban

governor
ammrado

grab
tam

grace
adom

gracious
a-ɔkyɛso

graduate
skuulwieni

grain
adibanamma

gramme
gram

grandchild
banana

grandfather
nanabanin

grandma
nanabaa

grape
bobeaba

grass
nkyɛkyɛre

grasshopper
abɛbɛw

grave
nnaa

gray

gon

grease
serade

great
kɛse

great-grandchild
nanasante twisoa

greed
adifudi

greedy
tumfuru

green
bun

greenish
abunabun

greet
kyia

greeting
nkyia

grief
awerɛhow

grieve
di yaw

grind
nyam

groin
ahaamu

ground
daade

groundnut
nkate

grove
pɔw

growth
nini

guard
weɔn

guava
aguabɛ

guest
hɔho

guest room
ahɔhodan

guide
gya ... kwan

guide
kwangyani

Guinea
Gini

Guinea-Bissau
Bisaw-Gini

guinea-fowl
akɔmfɛm

Guinean
Ginini

guitar
sanku

gun
turu

gunpowder
atuduru

gutter
gɔta

guy
ni nin

h

h

habit
suban

habitat
tenabea

had
nyaee

hair
hwi

haircut
tiriyi

half
fa

hall
asare

hallelujah
aleluya

hammer
hamɛr

hammock
apasante twi

hand
nsa

handkerchief
hankete

hang
sɛn

happen
si

happiness
anigye

happy
anigye-anigye

happy birthday
wo tiri nkwa o
happy new year
afehyia pa
harass
teetee
harbour
berano
hard
den
hardship
ahokyere
hare
adanko
harmattan
Ahanamanta
harvest
nnɔbaa
has
wɔ
hashtag
hahyetage
hassle
yere
hat
kyɛw
hate
kyiri
hatred
tan
Hausa
Hawosa
have
wɔ
have a hold on
de
hawk
bɔ ... tuutuu
hawk
akrɔma
he
ɔ
head
tiri
headache
tiripae
headgear
takua
heading
asɛmpɔw
headscarf
duukuu
heal
sa
healing
yaresa
health
akwahosan
heap
kuwu
hear
te
heard
teee
heart
akoma

heartburn
 aboyerɛw
hearth
 bukyia
heat
 hyew
heavy
 duruduru
hedgehog
 akrante
heel
 nantiri
heh
 wae
height
 korɔn
helicopter
 alikɔpta
helium
 hiliyɔm
hell
 samanade
hello
 ɛ te sɛn
helmsman
 kutoni
help
 boa
helper
 boafo
hemisphere
 kurukuruwafa
heptagon

 kwanɛn-suon
her
 ne
her
 no
herb
 ahahan
herbalist
 dunsini
here
 ha
here
 ha
herpes
 kore
herring
 eban
hers
 nede
hexagon
 kwanɛn-asia
hi
 agoo
hiccups
 kotiko
hide
 suma
highlife
 Haelaefe
highway
 kwantemfi
hill
 koko

him
no
himself
neho
hip
dwonku
hiplife
Heplaefe
hippopotamus
nsusono
his
ne
his
nede
history
abakɔsɛm
hit
bɔ
hmph
bɔyeɛ
hoe
asɔw
hold
kita
hole
tokuro
holiday
homeda
holy
krɔnkrɔn
home
fie
homeless

anenamfikyiri
hometown
kurowmu
honey
ɛwo
honeycomb
ɛwokyɛm
honour
hyɛ ... animunyam
honour
bu
hope
anidado
horn
ammɛn
horse
pɔnkɔ
hot
hyew
hotel
ahɔhofi
hour
dɔn
house
dan
housefly
wansena
how
sɛdea
how are you
ɛ te sɛn
how much
ahen

hug
 atuu
huge
 kuntann
human
 dasani
humankind
 adasa
humble
 ahobrɛase
humility
 ahobrɛase
hundred
 ɔha
hunger
 kɔm
hungry
 a-kɔm-de-no
hunter
 bɔmmɔni
hurry
 ka ... ho
husband
 kunu
hut
 pata
hydrogen
 haedrogyen
hydrogen
 haedrogyen
hyena
 pataku
hypocrisy

 nyaatwem
I
 me
i miss you
 me afe wo
idea
 adwenepɔw
ideal
 sema
idiot
 gyimini
if
 sɛ
if ... then
 sɛ ... a
Igbo
 Ibo
image
 mfonin
immediately
 prɛkopɛ
immerse
 nu
immigrant
 mamforani
impact
 nsesatumi
impertinence
 niyiano
important
 titiriw
impregnate
 yem

improvement
nkɔso

in
mu

in advance
prɛko

in fact
saana

in front
animu

in that case
ɛno de

inactive
tebɔɔ

incinerate
hyew

increase
dɔɔso

independence
fawohodi

India
Innia

Indian
Inniani

Indian
Innia

indictment
kwaadu

indigent
hiani

indigo
innigo

Indonesia

Innonihyia

Indonesian
Innonihyiani

infect
sane

infertile
saadwe

infinity
afebɔɔ

influence
nkɛntɛnso

information
niano

infrastructure
ahonyaguatiri

inheritance
adedi

inject
wɔ ... panne

injection
panne

injure
pira

ink
enke

inlaw
asew

insect
aboawa

inside
mu

inside
wɔ ... mu

insinuate
 keka
insult
 hyɛ ... ahoroba
insult
 ahoroba
insults
 ahorobahyɛ
integrate
 ka ... fra mu
intelligent
 adwenemutew
interest
 nsiho
internet
 intanɛte
interpreter
 kasakyerɛmuni
interrupt
 twa ... ano
intersection
 nkwanta
introduction
 nianim
investigation
 nhwehwɛmu
investment
 guatiri
iodine
 ayodiin
Iran
 Iran
Iranian

 Iranni
Iraq
 Irak
Iraqi
 Irakni
iron
 dade
is
 yɛ
Islam
 kramosom
Islamic
 kramo
island
 supruw
Israel
 Israɛl
Israeli
 Israɛlni
issue
 asɛm
it
 ɛ
Italy
 Italiya
its
 ne
Ivoirian
 Asommɛn Mpoanoni
ivory
 asommɛn
j
 gy

jaguar
 gyagowa
jail
 fiase
jama
 gyama
Jamaica
 Gyameika
James
 Yakobo
January
 Ɔpɛpɔn
Japan
 Gyapan
Japanese
 Gyapanni
jar
 toa
jaw
 nyepi
jeans
 gyinse
Jehovah
 Yehowa
jest
 gyimi
jester
 gyimi
Jesus
 Yesu
jewelry
 agudi
job

adwuma
John
 Yohanes
join
 bomu
joint
 pɔw
joke
 aserewsɛm
jollof
 dwɔlɔf
Jordan
 Jɔɔdan
Jordanian
 Jɔɔdanni
journalist
 samuni
journey
 akwantu
joy
 anigye
judge
 asɛnniini
judgement
 asɛnnii
July
 Ayɛwoho
jump
 huruw
June
 Ayɛwohomumu
junk
 nkukunkaka

just
kɛkɛ
just
ara
just
waa
justice
atɛntenenee
k
k
Kazakhstan
Kazakestan
Kazakhstani
Kazakestanni
keep
fa
kenkey
dɔkono
kente
kente
Kenya
Kenya
kept
faee
kerosene
kresiin
key
saafee
keyboard
kiibɔd
khakhi
kakii
khebab

kyinkyinga
kidnapping
nkyetɔn
kidney
saa
kill
ku
kilometer
kilomita
kind
sɛso
kindle
kua
kindness
ayamuyie
king
hen
kingdom
aheneman
kiss
few
kitchen
gyaade
knee
kotodwe
knife
sekan
knot
pɔw
know
nim
knowledge
nimdee

Kobina	Keregezestanni
Kwabena	**l**
Kofi	l
Kofi	**laboratory**
Kojo	labo
Kwadwo	**ladder**
kokonte	atwere
kokonte	**ladle**
kola nut	ti
bese	**ladle**
kolanut	kwanta
bese	**lady**
Komoros	awura
Kɔmɔrɔs	**lagoon**
Kongo	baka
Kongo	**lake**
koran	nsutae
koran	**lamb**
Kow	guamma
Kwaw	**lameness**
Kuwait	bubua
Kuweti	**lamentation**
Kuwaiti	kwadwom
Kuwetini	**land**
Kwame	asaase
Kwame	**land**
Kweku	kafamu
Kwaku	**landlord**
Kwesi	fiewura
Kwasi	**language**
Kyrgyzstan	kasa
Keregezestan	**lantern**
Kyrgyzstani	kannea

Lao
 Laosni
Laos
 Laos
lapse
 aniduado
laptop
 laptop
large
 kakraka
last
 a-ɛ-di-akyiri
last
 dea-ɛ-di-anim
lastborn
 abakyiba
late
 leeti
later
 akyiriyi
latrine
 duado
laugh
 serew
launder
 hohoro
law
 mmara
lawyer
 kasamafo
lay
 deda
laziness

anihaw
lazy
 taahɔbɛdi
lead
 di ... kan
lead
 summui
leader
 kwankyerɛni
leaf
 hataw
leak
 wini
lean on
 twere
learn
 sua
learner
 suani
leave
 gya
Lebanese
 Lɛbanɔnni
Lebanon
 Lɛbanɔn
ledge
 bamma
left
 bankum
left
 gyaee
leg
 nan

leisure
adagye
lemon
gurannsera
lend
fɛm
length
tenten
leniency
tirimummɔbɔr
lens
lɛnse
leopard
sebɔ
leper
kwatani
leprosy
kwata
Lesotho
Lisooto
lesson
suade
let
ma
letter
lɛtɛ
levy
tow
liar
kohwini
Liberia
Laeberia
Liberian

Laeberiani
liberty
ahofadi
library
nwomakorabea
Libya
Libia
Libyan
Libiani
lick
tafere
lid
mmuwado
lie
atoro
lie
di ... akohwi
life
bra
lifestyle
abrabɔ
lifetime
brabere
lift
ma ... do
lift
lefte
lift up
pagya
light
hann
lightning
aninam

lightweight
hare
like
sɛ
like
pɛ
like
tesɛ
lily
sukookoo
lime
ankama
line
hyɛe
Lingala
Lingala
link
lenke
lion
awennade
lip
anofamfa
lipbalm
anobam
lipstick
ahoɔfɛw anobam
liquid
nsunsu
liquor
nsa
listen
tie
listener

tieni
lithium
litiyɔm
litigant
mansotweni
litigate
twe manso
litigation
manso
little
ketewa
little
kakra
little by little
nkakrankakra
live
te
liver
brɛbo
living
tease
living-room
asado
lizard
ketew
loan
bosea
loan
bɔ ... bosea
lobster
bɔnkɔ
location
tebea

lock
krɔkrɔw
locust
aboadabi
lodge
asoɛe
log in
kɔ ... mu
log out
puei
logo
logo
loin
asen
London
Lɛnnɛn
long
tenten
longevity
ninkyɛre
look
hwɛ
look away
yi ... ani
loosen
baa ... mu
Lord
Awurade
lorry
lɔre
lose
hwere
lost

hwereee
loud
dededede
louse
dwuw
love
dɔ
love
dɔ
loyal
brɛbo
loyalty
brɛbode
luck
lɔk
lucky
lɔki
Luganda
Luganna
lump
tɔw
lung
hurututu
Luwo
Luwo
Luxembourg
Lakzemmɔg
Luxembourger
Lakzemmɔgni
luxury
ahotɔ
m
m

Maasai
 Maa
machine
 afiri
Madagascar
 Madagaska
madam
 eno
made
 yɛee
magazine
 magazin
maggot
 nsaamaa
magnesium
 maginisiyɔm
maid
 abaawa
maiden
 abaayewa
mail
 mel
main
 akotene
maintain
 hwɛ ... so yie
major
 pɔn
make
 yɛ
make love
 di ɔdɔ
Malagasy

Malagasi
malaria
 hurae
Malawi
 Malawi
Malawian
 Malawini
Malaysia
 Malehyia
Malaysian
 Malehyiani
Maldives
 Maldivs
Maldivian
 Maldivsni
male
 barima
Mali
 Mali
Malian
 Malini
mammy-truck
 annworogyeraase
man
 banin
manage
 hwɛ ... so
manager
 manegya
Manding
 Manning
manganese
 nkodwobo

mango
mango

manner
yɛbea

many
pii

map
mape

march
tow abasa

March
Ebɔw

marijuana
wii

Mark
akam

market
gua

marriage
aware

marry
ware

mass
nyo

master
wura

masticate
wosaw

mat
kɛtɛ

mathematics
nkontaabu

Matthew

Mateo

mattress
bɛr

Mauritania
Mɔritaniya

Mauritanian
Mɔritaniyani

Mauritian
Mɔrihyiɔsni

Mauritius
Mɔrihyiɔs

maximum
kɛsepaa

May
Asusow Aketeaba

maybe
gyama

me
me

mean
kyerɛsɛ

meaning
nkyerɛmu

measles
ntoburo

measure
sese

measure
nsusui

meat
nam

meet
hyia

meeting
nhyiamu
melon
fere
melon seed
akatewa
melt
nane
memorization
babadi
memorize
baba
memory
nkae
men
mmanin
mention
bɔ
mercy
ahummɔbɔ
mere
kwa
message
nkra
messengers
asomafo
messiah
mesia
met
hyiaee
metal
dade
metaphor

mɛtafɔ
metre
mita
mile
kwansin
milestone
mpɛmpɛnso
milk
merekye
millet
atoko
million
ɔpepem
mind
adwene
mine
mede
minimum
keteketepaa
ministry
minisitiri
minor
tia
mint
nunum
minute
sema
mirror
ahwehwɛ
miser
kyekyereteni
miserly
pɛpɛɛ

misfortune
asiane

miss
fe

miss
awuraa

missionary
asɛmpatrɛwni

missus
owurayere

mist
wanta

mistake
mfomso

mistress
awuraba

mix
fora

modern
abaeforo

moment
bere

Monday
Dwowda

money
sika

Mongolia
Mɔngolia

Mongolian
Mɔngoliani

monitor
mɔnita

monkey

adow

monster
kakae

month
bosoome

moon
bosoome

more
biom-so

more
bi ka ho

more than
sen

morning
anapa

Moroccan
Morokoni

Morocco
Moroko

morsel
trɔma

mortar
waduru

Moscovium
moskoveyɔm

Mosotho
Lisootoni

mosque
nkramodan

mosquito
ntontom

mother
maame

motorbike
moto
Motswana
Botswanani
mountain
bepɔw
mourner
befo
mouse
kura
moustache
mfemfem
mouth
ano
Mozambican
Mozammikni
Mozambique
Mozammik
mtchew
twee
much
tu
mud
apɔtɔbibiri
mudfish
adwen
multiplication
mmɔho
murder
awudi
murderer
wudini
mushroom

mmire
music
nnwom
musician
dwontoni
muslim
kramoni
mute
mumu
my
me
Myanma
Mayanmani
Myanmar
Mayanma
myself
meho
n
n
nail
dadewa
nail
awerɛw
name
din
Namibia
Namibia
Namibian
Namibiani
napkin
napken
nara
nara

nation
man
national
manina
nausea
abofon
near
bɛn
neck
kɔn
necklace
kɔnmuade
need
hia
need
hiade
needle
doroba
negative
kaw
neighbour
mpɔtamuni
neighbourhood
mpɔta
neon
neyɔn
Nepal
Nepɔl
Nepali
Nepɔlni
nephew
wɔfase
nerve

ahuon-ntini
nervous
nɛɛvɔs
net
asawu
network
nɛtewɛke
neutron
niwtrɔn
never
da
new
foforo
news
dawuru
newspaper
dawurubɔ-krataa
next
dea-ɛ-di-akyiri
niece
wɔfasewa
Niger
Nigyɛɛ
Nigeria
Alata
Nigerian
Alatani
Nigerien
Nigyɛɛni
night
anadwe
nightfall
adesaa

Nihonium
 nihoneyɔm
nine
 akron
nine persons
 baakron
nineteen
 du-akron
nineteenth
 dea-ɛ-tɔso-du-akron
ninety
 aduakron
nipple
 numfuano
nitrogen
 naetrogyen
no
 aaha
Noah
 Nowa
nobility
 ahenewa
noise
 dede
nominate
 hyɛ
nonagon
 kwanɛn-kron
nonsense
 nkwaseasɛm
noon
 wigyinae
normal

 saa ara
north
 atifi
North Korea
 Atifi Koria
North Korean
 Atifi Koriani
nose
 hwene
not have
 nni
nothing
 hwee
noun
 din
November
 Obubuo
novice
 abaeforo
now
 seisei
now
 afei
nowadays
 nnaansayi
nucleus
 niwklɔs
number
 kanee
nurse
 nɛɛse
nut
 dwe

oa
o

oar
tabon

oath
nsew

obedience
asotie

obey
yɛ ... asotie

obstacle
kwansiw

ocean
bosompo

octagon
kwanɛn-twe

October
Ahinime

of
ne

offering
ntoboa

office
ɔfese

often
taa

Oganesson
oganeson

oh
ao

oil
ngo

okay
yoo

okra
nkunuma

old
dadaw

old lady
aberewa

old man
akokora

Olympics
Olimpek

Oman
Oman

Omani
Omanni

on
do

one
koro

one
wɔ

one by one
nkorokoro

one person
baako

onion
anwew

only
nko

open
buei

oppose
tia

oppress
hyɛ ... do
oppression
ateetee
option
pade
or
anaa
orange
ɔrengye
orange
akutu
orphan
gyanka
ostentatious
hyɛpɛɛ
ostrich
sohori
other
biso
other side
noho
ouch
agyeei
our
hɛn
ours
hɛnne
ourselves
hɛnho
outdated
tetekwaa
outdoors

abowano
outside
abɔntene
outside
paado
outskirt
nkwantia
ovary
badwoa
oven
foonoo
overflow
yiri
overgrow
fuw
overturn
butuw
oware
ɔware
owe
de ... kaw
owl
patu
owner
wura
ox
kwaedu
oxygen
ɔksegyen
oxygen
ɔksegyen
oyster
adante

p
p
Pacific
Pasefek
pacify
pata
padlock
awur
page
fa
pail
asesawnsu
pain
yaw
painful
yaw
paint
akado
Pakistan
Pakestan
Pakistani
Pakestanni
palace
ahemfie
Palestine
Palestaen
Palestinean
Palestaenni
palm
nsaterɛ
palm
abɛ
palm kernel oil

adwengo
palmkernel
adwe
palmnut
abɛfua
palmnut soup
abɛnkwan
palmnut wool
abɛsɛntrɔw
palmwine
nsaefuw
pan
kyɛnse
pap
mpampa
papaya
bɔɔfrɛ
paper
krataa
parable
abɛbusɛm
paralysis
mmubui
parched
were
parent
tete
parent
baatan
parents
awofo
park
paake

parliament
mmrahyɛbagua
parrot
akoo
parsley
paasole
part
fa
partner
padi
party
ponto
pass
sen
pass by
nam
passport
paspɔte
password
ahintasɛmfua
paste
tare
pastor
sɔfo
path
anamɔnkwan
patience
abotare
patient
a-ɛ-wɔ-abotare
patient
yareni
patriotism

amannɔ
pay
tua
peace
asomudwoe
peacock
sukɔnkɔn
peck
sosɔw
pedestrian
nanteni
pedophile
awengaa
peel
huane
peel off
wae
peer
fɛ
pen
kyerɛwdua
pencil
pɛnsere
penis
kɔte
pentagon
kwanɛn-anum
people
nkorɔfo
pepper
muoko
perfect
pɛ

perfume
anowatar
period
bra
perjury
kontompo
perm
pɛɛmen
permanent
afebɔɔ
persecute
taataa
person
ni
pesewa
pɛsewa
pestle
wɔmma
pet
abɛbɛ
philanderer
asante twiiakaba
philanthropist
dɛefo
Philippines
Felepins
philosopher
nyansapɛni
philosophy
nyansapɛ
phlegm
ahɔre
phone

telefoon
phosphorus
fɔsefɔrɔs
photograph
foto
photograph
twa ... mfonin
physics
feseks
piano
adakabɛn
pick
bɔbo
pick up
sesaw
pie
paye
pierce
tuei
pig
prako
pigeon
asam
pigfeet
prakontwɛre
piglet
prakoba
pillar
tuntuma
pillow
sunni
pimple
mfoba

pinch
titi

pineapple
aborɔbɛ

pink
penke

pins and needles
nketenkete

pioneer
satwani

pipe
abuwa

pit
bɔn

pitch black
kebii

pitiable
mmɔbɔrwa

pitiful
mmɔbɔr

pito
pito

pizza
piza

place
bea

plague
yaredɔm

plan
paam

plan
apaam

plane

aroplen

planet
planɛte

plank
taabow

plant
dua

plant
haban

plantain
borɛde

plaster
plasta

plastic
plastek

play
agoro

play
di agoro

please
me pa wo kyɛw

pleasure
anisɔ

pledge
abasode

plentiful
bum

plenty
babiree

pluck
tew

pocket
bɔtɔ

poem
anwensɛm

point
pɔw

poisonous
kankabi

poke
puti

police
poliisi

political party
amanɛkuw

politician
amanɛni

politics
amanɛ

pomade
nkuto

poop
tiafi

poor
wesee

porcupine
kɔtɔkɔ

pork
prakonam

porpoise
ntui

porridge
kooko

port
hyɛn-gyinabea

porter
kaya

position
dibew

post office
posɔfese

pot
kutu

potassium
potaseyɔm

potty
kuraba

pound
siw

pound
pɔɔn

pour
huei

poverty
hia

powder-keg
kwadum

powerful
tumfo

praise
yi ... ayɛw

praise
ayɛw

pray
bɔ mpae

prayer
mpae

preacher
asɛmpasante twiyi

preface
nianim
pregnancy
ninsɛn
prejudice
ahihunu
preparation
ahoboa
preparations
ahoboaboa
prepare
ben
preservation
akora
preservative
akyekyennuru
preserve
kora
president
ɔmampanin
press
mia
pretend
hyɛ da
pretty
fɛwfɛw
price
bo
pride
ahantan
prince
ɔhenebanin
princess

ɔhenebabea
print
prente
printer
timtimni
priority
adehiapaa
prison
fiade
privacy
kokoamusɛm
private
kokoa
privately
nkokoamu
problem
akwammew
proceed
kɔr
procession
santene
proclamation
dawurubɔ
procrastination
mmɔtohɔ
product
guade
professor
kyerɛkyerɛni
profit
mfaso
programme
dwumadi

project
adwumatɔw
promise
bɔ ... anohoba
promise
anohoba
pronoun
dinhyɛananmu
proof
adanse
prop
wɔw
property
agyapade
prophesy
hyɛ nkɔm
prophet
kɔmfo
proprietor
adwumawura
prosperity
yiedi
prostitute
ahyeawo
protect
bɔ ... ho ban
protection
bammɔ
proton
protɔn
proverb
bɛ
Proverbs

Mbɛbusɛm
prudence
nyansahobrɛase
prudent
nyansahobrɛaseno
psychology
saekɔ
public
bagua
puff-adder
nanka
pull
twe
pungently
kankan
punish
twe ... aso
pupil
aniwamma
puppet
koliko
purchase
totɔ
pure
mapa
purple
berdum
purpose
tirimupɔw
pursue
tiw
push
pia

puzzle
abrɔme
python
onin
q
kw
Qatar
Kataa
Qatari
Kataani
quake
wosow
quality
kamayɛ
quantity
dodow
quarrel
atwɛre
quarter
famufa
queen
hemmaa
question
asɛmmisa
quick
ntɛm
quiet
dinn
r
r
rabbit
asoasoa
race
mmirika
radiation
adwumatumipuw
radio
kasafiri
rag
ntomagow
railway
ketekekwan
rain
nsutɔ
rainbow
nyankontɔn
rainy season
nsutɔbere
raise
pagya
raisin
asikyireamma
ran
tuee nguan
ransom
asatiri
rap
kasahare
rape
to ... monaa
rascal
azaa
rat
kusi
raucously
kwaakwaa

razor
yinnam
reach
du
reach a final milestone
so
read
kan
reading
akenkan
ready
krado
real
ankasa
realm
amansuon
rear
nyɛn
rearguard
nkyidɔm
reason
siantiri
rebel
tuatewni
rebellion
tuatew
recover
te apɔw
rectangle
kwanɛn-nan
recurring
kɔannkɔ
red

kɔkɔɔ
reduce
tew
reflection
husu
refuge
guankɔbea
refugee
amamforani
region
mantaw
regret
nu ... hu
regret
nuhu
reign
di ... hene
reject
pow
rejoice
di dɛw
relative
busuani
remain
tena
remainder
nkae
remember
kae
remind
bɔ ... nkae
remorse
anuho

remove
 yi
rent
 dan-kaw
repeat
 si ... do
repent
 nu ... ho
repentance
 nnuho
replace
 hyɛ ... ananmu
replacement
 nhyɛananmu
report
 amanneɛ
request
 bisade
requester
 bisafo
rescue
 gye
resemble
 sɛ
reside
 te
respect
 bu
respect
 anidi
respond
 bua
response

 ngyeso
responsibility
 asɛde
rest
 gye ... ahome
restaurant
 adidibea
resurrection
 wunyane
return
 san
Reunion
 Reyuniɔn
reveal
 yi ... adi
revelation
 yikyerɛ
revival
 nkenyan
revive
 kenyan
rheumatism
 nwewee
rice
 moo
rich
 bafuu
riddle
 abisaa
right
 nifa
rights
 nninoa

ring
  kawa
ringworm
  eyam
ripen
  bere
rival
  kora
rivalry
  koratwe
river
  nsutene
road
  kwan
roam
  kyima
roast
  toto
robe
  batakeri
rock
  hinhim
rock
  botan
rocket
  rɔkɛte
Romans
  Romafo
roof
  dampare
roof
  kur
room

  pia
roost
  buwa
root
  ntini
rope
  kyehoma
rose
  roosu
rot
  prɔw
row
  kwan
row
  kyerɛpɛn
royal
  adehye
rule
  mmara
rum
  mmorɔnsa
rump
  pah
run
  tu nguan
Russia
  Rahyia
Russian
  Rahyiani
Rwanda
  Rwanna
Rwandan
  Rwannani

s
 s

sabotage
 bɔ ... aboro

sabotage
 aboro

sack
 kotoku

sacrifice
 afɔre

sacrilege
 busu

sad
 mmɔbɔ-mmɔbɔ

sadness
 awerɛhow

safe travels
 kwanso brɛbrɛ

safety
 nkwabammɔ

said
 seee

salad
 ahahan

salt
 nkyene

salted fish
 koobi

salvation
 nkwagye

same
 pɛr

sand

 anhwea

sang
 towee

Santomean
 Sao Tome na Prensepeni

Sao Tome and Principe
 Sao Tome na Prensepe

Saturday
 Memeneda

sauce
 abomu

saucepan
 saspan

Saudi Arabia
 Sawdi Arabia

Saudi Arabian
 Sawdi Arabiani

savant
 nyansani

save
 sie

saviour
 agyenkwa

saw
 huee

saw
 sradaa

say
 se

say goodbye
 kra

scald
 hyehyew

scale
bon
scanner
skana
scar
dɛm
scarce
na
scarcity
na
scarecrow
birekutu
scarlet
serdaa
scary
hu
scatter
pete
scholarship
skɔlahyepe
school
sukuu
schooling
skuulkɔ
science
sayense
scissors
apaso
scoop
saw
score
hyɛ
scorn

atwetwe
scorpion
nyankoma-ketebowa
Scotland
Skɔtasaase
scrape
twerɛw
scripture
kyerɛwsɛm
scrub
twitwiw
sea
po
search
hwehwɛ
second
dea-ɛ-tɔso-abien
second
pare
secret
asiesɛm
security
ahobammɔ
see
hu
see ... off
gya ... kwan
seed
amma
seek
hwehwɛ
Sekondi
Sekunne

select
 yi
self
 ho
selfishness
 pɛsɛmenkomenya
sell
 tɔn
seller
 tɔnni
send
 soma
Senegal
 Senegal
Senegalese
 Senegalni
sense
 te ... nka
sentence
 sɛntɔw
September
 Ɛbɔ
serious
 anibere
servant
 akowa
servanthood
 nkoasom
serves you right
 ɔtwea
service
 som
Seselwa

 Sehyɛlsni
settle
 soɛe
seven
 asuon
seven persons
 baasuon
seventeen
 du-asuon
seventy
 aduasuon
several
 ahorow
sew
 pam
sex
 mpamugoro
sex education
 bragoro
sexy
 beree
Seychelles
 Sehyɛls
sh
 hy
shade
 pata
shame
 anito
shame
 hurow
shape
 bɔbea

share
kyɛfa

share
kyɛ

share bed with husband
da nkunkyire

sharpen
sew

she
ɔ

sheabutter
nku

sheep
guan

shell
bon

shield
kyɛm

shine
hyeren

ship
pohyɛn

shirt
hyɛɛte

shit
nyee

shoe
asopatere

Shona
Hyeɔna

shoot
tow

shop

adwumabea

shopping
gua

short
tiatia

shorts
nika

shoulder
batiri

shout
keka mu

show
kyerɛ

show ... pity
hu ... mmobɔr

shrimp
sɛsɛw

shut
mua

shut down
pɔn

shy
a-ɔ-fɛre-ade

shyness
fɛre

sibling
nua

sickness
yareba

side
afa

Sierra Leone
Siɛra Leon

Sierra Leonean
 Siɛra Leonni
sigh
 si ... nkrum
sighing
 nkrumsi
sign
 ahyɛnsew
signpost
 nkwantabisa
silence
 kommyɛ
silent
 komm
silicon
 selekɔn
silk
 serekye
silk cotton tree
 anina
silver
 dwetɛ
silver
 dwetɛ
sin
 bɔne
since
 fiti
sing
 tow
sing jama
 hye gyama
Singapore

 Sengapɔɔ
Singaporean
 Sengapɔɔni
singing
 nnwomtow
singleton
 bafua
sink
 senke
sink
 mem
sir
 owura
siren
 nino
sister
 akyerɛbaa
sit
 tena
six
 asia
six persons
 baasia
sixteen
 du-asia
sixty
 aduasia
skill
 adeyɛ
skin
 honamani
skirt
 sekɛɛte

skull
 tidwereba
sky
 wimu
slap
 bɔ ... asowa mu
slate
 sirete
slave
 donkɔ
slavegirl
 afenaa
sleep
 da
sleep crust
 mpe
sleep tight
 da yie
sleepiness
 anikom
slept
 daee
slice
 twitwa
slim
 hweaa
slip
 terew
slippers
 kyeale wote
slowly
 bɔkɔɔ
sluggard

 kwaadonto
slurp
 hwirow
small
 kete
smaller
 kuma
smallest
 kakraba
smash
 bubu
smell
 hua
smell
 nka
smile
 serew
smoke
 wusiw
smoothen
 kokwa
snail
 nwa
snake
 abowatena
snatch
 hwim
sneeze
 hunti
snore
 huam nkrɔm
snoring
 nkrɔm

snow
nsukyerɛma
snuff
asera
so
nti
so there
oyiwa
soaked
fɔkyee
soap
samina
sock
asetaagyee
sodium
sodiyɔm
sofa
sofa
soft
gowgow
soften
gow
soldier
sordaani
sole
korotee
sole
ananade
solemn
krɔn
solid
dennene
solution

anoaduru
Somali
Somali
Somalia
Somalia
Somalian
Somaliani
some
bi
some
bi
somebody
obi
something
biribi
something
biribi
sometimes
ɛ-tɔ-da-bi-a
somewhere
baabi
son
babanin
song
nnwom
soon
seisei
soot
huntuma
sorcery
bayi
sore
kuru

sorry
kosɛ

soul
kra

sound
dede

soup
nkwan

south
anaafo

South Africa
Abibir Anaafo

South African
Abibir Anaafoni

South Korea
Anaafo Koria

South Korean
Anaafo Koriani

South Sudan
Sudan Anaafo

South Sudanese
Sudan Anaafoni

space
spese

spade
sofi

Spain
Spen

Spanish
Spen kasa

Spanish
Spen kasa

spank

hwe

spanner
sopana

spatula
tah

speak
ka

spear
pea

special
sornonko

specific
pɔtee

spectacles
ahwehwɛaniwa

spectator
bɛhwɛadeni

speed
hare

spider
ananse

spin-top
ntɛ

spinal cord
kratebiew-ahuon-ntini

spine
kratebiew

spinning top
ntɛ

spirit
honhom

spittle
ntafi

split
  pae ... mu
spokesperson
  kyeame
sponge
  sapɔw
sponsor
  kyigyinani
spoon
  atere
spoor
  kyenan
sport
  asante twisi-agodi
spouse
  hokafo
spread
  trɛw
spread out
  sɔw
spring
  fefɛwbere
springwater
  mmasu
sprout
  fefuw
spy
  kwanserani
spy
  sera akwan
squabbles
  wentwiwentwi
squat

  kotow
squeeze
  kyere
squeeze drum
  donno
squirrel
  amokua
Sri Lanka
  Sri Lanka
Sri Lankan
  Sri Lankani
stab
  wɔ
stadium
  stediyɔm
staff
  poma
stair
  atwede
stamina
  akomaden
stamp
  tim
stand
  gyina
star
  soroma
start
  hyɛ ... ase
startle
  bɔ birim
state
  gyinabew

state
to adi
station
stehyɛn
steal
wia
steer
kutow
step
tia
step-child
abanoma
stew
frɔwee
steward
ankɔbea
stick
duaba
still
dado
stimulate
ka ... hyew
stinginess
ayamuɔwen
stink
bɔn
stinking fish seasoning
mɔmɔe
stir
nunu
stomach-ache
yamukaw
stone

boba
stool
akentengua
stop
gyinabea
store
setɔɔ
storehouse
adekoradan
storey building
abansoro
storm
ahum
story
anansesɛm
stove
bukyia
straight
tee
straighten
tene
stranger
nanaben
stream
asuba
street
setiiti
strength
ahoɔden
strengthen
hyɛ ... den
stretch
twe ... mu

string
ahoma

strip off
worɔw

stripe
sensan

striped
nsensansensan

strive
bɔ ... mmɔden

stroll
mpasar

stroll
pasar

strong
ɔberan

strongly
ketee

student
sukuuni

studio
studiyo

study
sua

stumble
fintiw

stump
kukuw

stupid
fon

submarine
nsuadehɛn

subtract
yi ... so

subtraction
nifimu

success
nim

such as this
basiaba

suck
hwiruow

suckle
num

Sudan
Sudan

Sudanese
Sudanni

suddenly
awerɛfirimu

sue
saman

suffer
hu amanne

suffering
amannehu

sugar
asikyire

sugarcane
ahwede

suicide
hoku

suit
suutu

suitcase
potumantu

sulfur
sɔlfa
summary
sin
summer
ahuhurobere
summit
atifi
sun
awia
Sunday
Kwasida
sunny
awiaawia
sunrise
apuei
sunset
atɔe
supply
amade
support
fua
supporter
kyiritaani
surf
ber
surpass
kyɛn
surprise
ahobow
surround
twa ... ho hyia
sushi

suhyi
Swahili
Swahili
swallow
mene
swallow
akyemfowa
swam
boroee
sway
him
Swazi
Swazilanneni
Swaziland
Swazilanne
swear
ka ... ntam
sweep
pra
sweet
dɛw
sweet potato
santom
sweetheart
nwewe
swell
hono
swift
annkadaade
swim
boro
swing
adenne

switch on
  sɔ
symbol
  adinkra
Syria
  Siria
Syrian
  Siriani
syringe
  bɛntoa
t
  t
t-shirt
  tiihyɛɛte
table
  pon
tail
  dua
tail
  tɛw
Taiwan
  Taewan
Taiwanese
  Taewanni
Tajik
  Tajekestanni
Tajikstan
  Tajekestan
take
  fa
take care
  hwɛ ... yie
take hold of

  de ... mu
Takoradi
  Takorade
talk
  kasa
talking drum
  atumpan
tall
  tenten
Tano
  Tanɔ
Tanzania
  Tanzania
Tanzanian
  Tanzaniani
tap
  paepe
tarantula
  kyɛfo
taste
  ka wo ano
tattered
  pamsam
taxi
  taksi
tea
  tii
teach
  kyerɛ
team
  nnɔboakuw
tear
  tew

tear
 aninsu
teardrop
 aninsuwa
tease
 di ... ho fɛw
technical
 adwin
teenage pregnancy
 kyiribra
teenager
 abasirwa
teeth
 se
telescope
 kyikyi
television
 tɛlɛvihyɛn
tell
 ka
temple
 asɔredan
ten
 du
Tennessine
 tɛnɛsaene
tense
 kabea
termite
 mfɔte
test
 tɛ
testament

ahyɛmu
testimony
 dase
testis
 ntɔhwɛ
Tetrapleura tetraptera
 prɛkɛsɛ
Thai
 Taelannni
Thailand
 Taelann
than
 kyɛn
thank
 da ... ase
thank you
 me da wo ase
thanks
 medaase
thanks
 aseda
thanksgiving
 nnaase
that
 a-ɔ
that
 dɛm
that
 a
that person
 ni dɛm
that thing
 ade dɛm

the
no

the other day
nnaano

the other time
nnaano

the thing
ade no

their
hɔn

theirs
wɔnne

them
hɔn

themselves
hɔnho

then
nna

there
hɔ

there
hɔ

these
yinom

these
yi

they
wɔ

thief
awi

thigh
serɛ

thin

feaa

thing
ade

things
nneɛmma

think
dwene

thinking
adwennwene

thirst
nsukɔm

thirteen
du-abiasa

thirty
aduasa

this
ni

this
weyi

thorn
nsɔe

those
seyi

though
kaansa

thought
adwenkyerɛ

thought
dweneee

thousand
apem

thousands
mpempem

threat
mpuw
three
abiasa
three persons
baasa
thrive
dɔre
throat
mene
throne
ahenegua
throw
tow
throw away
tow ... gu
thumb
kokromoti
thumbnail
mfoniwaa
thunder
aprannaa
thunderbolt
senamammo
Thursday
Yawda
tick
summɔre
ticket
tikiti
tidy
siesie
tie

kyekyere
tie
tae
tie-and-dye
tae-n-dae
tiger
gyasaaboafo
tigernut
atadwe
tightly
dennennnene
tile
tayaa
time
mmere
times
mpɛn
timetable
mmerenhyehyɛe
tin
konko
tiny
ketekete
tire
brɛ
tiredness
brɛ
tithe
taete
title
abɔdin
Titus
Tito

to
kɔdu
to-and-fro
akɔneaba
tobacco
tawa
today
nnɛ
toddler
akwadaa
toe
nansoa
toffee
tɔfe
Togo
Togo
Togolese
Togoni
toilet
tiefi
toilet roll
tiefi krataa
told
kaee
tomato
ntos
tomorrow
ɔkyena
tongue
tɛkyerɛma
too
dodow
too much

dodow
tooth
se
toothache
kakaw
toothbrush
sedua
toothpaste
seduru
tortoise
akyekyerɛ
torture
ninyanne
total
ninara
totally
koraa
touch
ka
tough
wensee
tour
nsrahwɛ
towel
antuhu
tower
abantenten
town
kurow
trade
bata
trade
di bata

trader
adetɔnni
trading
batadi
tradition
amammrɛ
traffic
trafeke
trailblazer
kannini
train
kyerɛ
train
keteke
traitor
mammɔeni
transform
dane
translate
kyerɛ ... mu
transportation
akwantunhyehyɛe
travel
tu kwan
traveller
kwantuni
tray
apampa
treason
amammɔe
treasure
akorade
tree

dua
tremble
popo
trembling
ahopopo
trend
kɔbea
triangle
kwanɛn-sa
trick
nkonyaa
trillion
ɔpepem-ɔpepem
trinity
baasakoro
trinket
afɛfɛde
trip
nkɔsan
triplets
ntansa
triumph
di ... nkonim
trouble
abɛbrɛsɛ
trouser
trɔsa
truck
trɔke
true
ampa
truly
ampaara

trumpet
totorobɛnto
trust

trust
ahotoso
truth
nokware
try
trae
ts
ts
tuberculosis
nsamanwa
Tuesday
Benada
tumbler
tɔmmɛr
Tunisia
Tunihyia
Tunisian
Tunihyiani
turbulent
kyikyiikyi
Turk
Tɛɛkini
Turkey
Tɛɛki
turkey
krakun
Turkmen
Tɛkemɛnestanni
Turkmenistan
Tɛkemɛnestan
turn off
dum
turpentine
takontaar
turtle
nsu-akyekyerɛ
Tuvalu
Tuvalu
tweet
tuwiite
twelve
du-abien
twenty
aduonu
Twi
Twi
twig
duabaa
twin
ata
twins
ntafo
twist
kyim
two
abien
two persons
baanu
type
taepe
type
su

tyre
taae

u
u

Uganda
Yuganna

Ugandan
Yugannani

ugly
akyere

ukelele
ukelele

Ukraine
Yukren

Ukrainean
Yukrenni

umbrella
akatawia

unappreciativeness
aniannsɔ

unburden
soɛ

uncle
wɔfa

under
ase

under
ase

understand
te ... ase

underwear
pieto

undesirable

tan

unfamiliar
yɛnnhubida

ungrateful
boniayɛ

union
nkabomkuw

unique
a-ɛ-da-mu-soronko

unit
yunete

unite
ka ... bom

United States of America
Amɛreka Amankuw

unity
koroyɛ

university
suapɔn

unkempt
basabasa

unless
kyedɛ

unnecessary
gyengyɛn

until
kɔsidɛ

up
soro

upright
tenenee

upstairs
abansoro

urinate
gu nsu
urine
gunsu
Ururimi
Ururimi
us
hɛn
use
yuso
useless
funu
user
dehye
utterly
pɔtɔɔ
Uzbek
Uzebɛkestanni
Uzbekistan
Uzebɛkestan
v
v
vacation
akwanma
vaccinate
bota
vacuum
vakum
vagina
twɛ
valiant
katakyi
valley

bɔnsa
value
sommo
van
trɔtrɔ
vase
hyera
vegetable oil
angoa
vehicle
hyɛn
vein
ntini
Venezuela
Venizuwela
Venezuelan
Venizuwelani
venom
bɔre
verandah
nkrannaa
verb
nyɛe
verse
nkyekyɛmu
version
vɛɛhyɛn
very
paa
very desirable
akɔnnɔakɔnnɔ
very much
papaapa

vibrate
hihim
vice
nneboneyɛ
vice-president
mankrado
victor
nkunimdini
victory
nkonim
video
vidio
Vietnam
Viyɛtnam
Vietnamese
Viyɛtnamni
village
akuraase
vine
bobe
violet
vaelɛt
virtue
papayɛ
vision
daakyeadehu
visit
sera
vitality
nkwa
vodka
vodka
voice

nne
volume
volum
vomit
fe
vomit
fe
vote
tow aba
voting
ammatow
vulture
pɛtɛ
w
w
waache
waakye
waah
ngaa
wailing
abooboo
waist
sisiw
wait
tweon
waiter
somfo
wake
nyan
wake up
nyan
walk
nantew

walk about
 nenam
wall
 afaban
walnut
 aborɔdwe
want
 pɛ
war
 ako
warhorn
 akobɛn
warn
 bɔ … kɔkɔ
warning
 kɔkɔ
warrior
 katakyi
warriors
 asafo
was
 yɛee
wasp
 kotokrodo
waste
 kwa
wasted
 gyan
watch
 hwɛ
watch
 wate
water

nsu
water yam
 afasew
watermelon
 anamuna
wave
 asorɛkye
way
 kwan
we
 yɛ
weak
 mmrɛw
weakness
 mmrɛwyɛ
wealth
 ahonya
weapon
 akode
wear
 hyɛ
weather
 wɛda
weave
 wene
weaverbird
 akyem
web
 ntentan
website
 wɛbsaete
wed
 yɛ … ayeforo

wedding
ayeforohyia

Wednesday
Wukuda

wee hours
asuom

weed
dɔw

week
dapɛn

weigh
kari

weight
duru

welcome
akɔaba

well
yie

well
bura

well done
ayekoo

wellbeing
yiyeyɛ

went
kɔee

were
yɛee

west
anee

Western Sahara
Sahara Anee

Western Saharan
Sahara Aneeni

wet
fɔwee

wet season
Asusow

whale
bonso

what
dɛn

wheat
awifua

wheel
hwiir

when
abere a

where
hemfa

which
bɛn

whine
winwin

whip
abaa

whistle
abɛn

white
fitaa

who
woana

whoa
dɛm

whole year
afehyia

whose
 woana ne
why
 adɛn
wicked
 tibɔne
wickedness
 tirimuden
wide
 yantamm
widowed
 kuna
widower
 kunafo
widowhood
 kuna
width
 trɛtrɛ
wield
 kukuru
wife
 yere
wifi
 waefae
wild
 ya
will
 pɛ
win
 di ... nim
wind
 mframa
window

 fɛnsere
windy
 mframamframa
wine
 bobe nsa
wing
 taban
winter
 awɔwbere
wipe
 pepa
wisdom
 nyansa
wise
 nyansanansa
witch
 anɛn-basia
witchcraft
 anɛn
with
 nye
withdraw
 twe
witness
 daseni
wizard
 anɛn-banin
wolf
 mali-kraman
Wolof
 Wɔlɔf
woman
 baa

womb
awode

women
mmaa

won
diee ... nim

wonder
nwanwa

wood
nnua

woodpigeon
bireku

word
kasafua

work
yɛ adwuma

work
adwuma

worker
dwumayɛni

working
adwumayɛ

workshop
adwimmea

world
wiade

worldliness
anibuei

worm
sunsuma

worry
haw

worship
som

wow
wao

wriggle
pepere

wring
kyin ... mu

wrist
abakɔn

write
kyerɛw

x
ks

xylophone
adakabɛn

xylopia
hwentea

y
y

Yaa
Yaa

yam
bayere

yard
adiwo

Yaw
Yaw

yawn
hram

yaws
dobɛ

yeah
ae

year
afe

yearly
afeafe

yell
tea mu

yellow
akoangoa

Yemen
Yɛmɛn

Yemeni
Yɛmɛnni

yes
aane

yesterday
nneda

yet
nso

Yoruba
Yoruba

you
wo

you
hom

you
e

you
hom

young
abrampa

young boy
aberantewa

young man
aberante

your
wo

your
hom

yours
homde

yourself
woho

yourselves
moho

youth
mmerantebere

z
dz

Zambia
Zammia

Zambian
zammiani

zebra
masae-pɔnkɔ

zero
hweeara

Zimbabwe
Zemmabuwe

Zimbabwean
Zemmabuweni

zip
zep

zoo
zu

Akan kasahorow Library

ak.kasahorow.org/app/l

help+ak@kasahorow.org

Made in the USA
Middletown, DE
11 June 2021

41890487R00121